Cultural Portraits: Japan and the US

Justin Charlebois   Atsushi Sakuma

KINSEIDO

Kinseido Publishing Co., Ltd.
3-21 Kanda Jimbo-cho, Chiyoda-ku,
Tokyo 101-0051, Japan

Copyright © 2015 by Justin Charlebois
        Atsushi Sakuma

All rights reserved. No part of this publication may be reproduced, stored in a retrieval system, or transmitted, in any form or by any means, electronic, mechanical, photocopying, recording or otherwise, without the prior permission of the publisher.

First published 2015 by Kinseido Publishing Co., Ltd.

Cover design Takayuki Minegishi
Text design   Nampoosha Co., Ltd.
Illustrations   Saori Otsuka

音声ファイル無料ダウンロード

https://www.kinsei-do.co.jp/download/3998

この教科書で DL 00 の表示がある箇所の音声は、上記 URL または QR コードにて無料でダウンロードできます。自習用音声としてご活用ください。

- ▶ PC からのダウンロードをお勧めします。スマートフォンなどでダウンロードされる場合は、
  ダウンロード前に「解凍アプリ」をインストールしてください。
- ▶ URL は、検索ボックスではなくアドレスバー（URL 表示欄）に入力してください。
- ▶ お使いのネットワーク環境によっては、ダウンロードできない場合があります。

◎ CD 00 左記の表示がある箇所の音声は、教室用 CD（Class Audio CD）に収録されています。

はしがき

　今日では、情報機器が普及し、誰でも様々な情報を必要な時に、いつでも触れることができるようになりました。海外の事柄についても同様ですが、この時に外国語、特に英語をある程度使いこなせれば、情報の理解を深めることができます。

　英語を学習する際には、単語の意味やイディオム、文法上の知識、さらには正しい発音とイントネーションを身に付けることが重要です。英語学習者の誰でも、このことに多くの努力を傾注しています。しかし、日本語についてもあてはまることですが、言葉が大きな意味を持つのは、言葉が活き活きしているからです。別な言い方をしたら、言葉に話者の意図が十分に込められた時に、言葉は活きたものになります。話者の意図には、まずは言葉が、次に話者の身振り、手振り、さらに広い意味では文化的要因が関わっています。

　本書では、言葉としての英語の理解を深めることを一義的な狙いとしていますが、さらに、この英語が使われているアメリカの文化を日本文化と比較しながら、その特徴を理解し、さらに日本人が普段は解っていると思っている自国文化についても改めて考えられるようになっています。

　本書では、まず、アメリカの大学生の学習や生活の仕方を学び、今日のアメリカ人がどのような家庭生活や食生活を送っているかが理解できるようになっています。さらに、アメリカ文化の特徴である個人主義がどのように形成されてきたのかを、若者のパーティーやデートを通じて見ていきますので、今日の若者がどのような問題に直面しているのかも理解できます。この時に日本文化との比較も行っていますので、日米の文化的違いも鮮明になります。日本文化には形式を重んじ、その形式こそが日本文化の特徴にもなっていますが、アメリカ文化には形式に拘るところがないことが理解できます。コミュニケーションを文化的文脈との関連で研究したのは、アメリカの文化人類学者のE・ホールですが、本書でも彼の論述を基にしながら、アメリカ文化が一元的でないことが理解できるようになっています。最後に、今日の世界的傾向として情報機器の普及がありますが、情報機器を通じたコミュニケーションには、これまでとは違った諸問題が派生してきていて、このことは英語学習の面でもあてはまることであり、英語学習上でどのようなことに注意を向けるべきかについて述べられています。

　このように本書は、英語や英語によるコミュニケーションを学習する上での諸問題を想定して、日本の英語学習者がアメリカ文化、特にアメリカの若者の文化の中で活きた英語を身に付けられるようにしています。本書を通じて、多くの人が英語を楽しく学び、アメリカ文化の今日的特徴を理解し、さらには日本文化について客観的な視点から分析して、その特徴を外国から日本を訪れる方々に英語で説明できるようになることを願っています。

著　者

Contents

Unit 1 ◆ College Life 1

Unit 2 ◆ Family Life 6

Unit 3 ◆ Food Culture 11

Unit 4 ◆ Holidays 16

Unit 5 ◆ Individualism 21

Unit 6 ◆ Socializing at Parties 26

Unit 7 ◆ Dating and Romance 31

Unit 8 ◆ Pluralistic Society 36

Unit 9 ◆ Degree of Formality 41

Unit 10 ◆ Volunteerism 46

Unit 11 ◆ Context and Communication 51

Unit 12 ◆ Non-Verbal Communication 56

Unit 13 ◆ Debate 61

Unit 14 ◆ Religion 66

Unit 15 ◆ Computers and Communication 71

Unit 1

College Life

アメリカの大学生活がどのようなものなのかについて、日本の多くの人には入学は簡単でも卒業は難しい位の印象しかないと思いますので、実態を見てみることにしましょう。これからアメリカの大学に入って勉強をするつもりで読んでみると、いろいろなことに気がつくかと思います。また、勉学以外の学生生活にも注意を向け、学生同士の英語の会話にも日本語とは異なる言語上の特徴が出てくることにも着目しましょう。

DL 02　CD1-02

Vocabulary Quiz

次の語句の意味を a. ～ j. から選び、（　　）内に記号を記入しましょう。

1. prominent institution　（　）　　a. 感じのよい
2. academic reputation　（　）　　b. 未成年の飲酒
3. formidable endeavor　（　）　　c. 褒め言葉
4. interactive　（　）　　d. 学問上の評判
5. campus dormitory　（　）　　e. 謙遜
6. pleasant　（　）　　f. 血のにじむような努力
7. underage drinking　（　）　　g. 卓越した組織
8. compliment　（　）　　h. 対話者
9. modesty　（　）　　i. 学内寮
10. interlocutor　（　）　　j. 対話式の

Reading

太字の語句に注意して、以下の英文を読みましょう。

1　College and university admissions requirements are less demanding in the US than they are in Japan. While the most **prominent institutions** are very difficult to gain admission, other schools are less competitive. Nevertheless, regardless of **academic reputation**, graduation from a school is a **formidable endeavor**. Therefore, students spend tremendous amounts of time studying and preparing for classes.

2　Students are referred to as freshmen, sophomores, juniors, and seniors, taking an average of four to five classes per semester. One class meets for three hours and instructors assign a good deal of homework. Whereas larger classes are usually taught in a lecture format, smaller classes are more discussion, group-work based and **interactive**. Instructors expect students to not only complete the homework but also actively participate in the class.

3　Many students enter colleges or universities that are far from their hometowns, so they live in a **campus dormitory** ("dorm"). Most dorms do not have kitchens, so students eat their meals in the residential dining halls. Socialization often originates from the dorm as well. Students eat meals or order food with their friends, watch movies, and hang out in others' dorm rooms. Since students' academic and social life occurs at school, there are many opportunities to develop friendships. While Americans are very friendly and **pleasant**, cultivating friendships requires exerting effort and taking the initiative.

4　College students do a variety of activities in their leisure time. Some students get involved with clubs, organizations, religious groups, or athletics, and other students are engaged in part-time employment. Employment is a necessity for some students to offset their education-related expenses. Most campuses have fitness centers which have a reasonable membership fee. Although twenty-one is the legal drinking age, **underage drinking** is prevalent in most college towns. Socializing in bars is a popular social activity, but it is socially acceptable for students to abstain from alcohol consumption. Other popular activities include dating, dining out, hanging out with friends, and watching movies.

5　In social interaction, Japanese students will inevitably notice how college-aged students typically compliment each other. Many Japanese experience difficulty formulating appropriate **compliment** responses. As Japanese culture values **modesty**, Japanese compliment responses are normally self-deprecatory.

The correct way to formulate a compliment response is to initially accept the compliment and then mitigate it with an explanation. As equality is valued in American culture, the mitigation emphasizes the **interlocutors'** equal relationship. In contrast, Japanese relationships are typically hierarchically organized, so a speaker emphasizes his or her own inferiority and highlights the interlocutor's superiority.

Notes

lecture format「講義形式」 dining hall「食堂」 hang out「頻繁に行く」 exerting「力を尽くした」 be engaged in「従事する」 offset「埋め合わせる」 abstain from「控える」 compliment response「ほめ言葉への応答」 self-deprecatory「自分を卑下する」 mitigate「和らげる」 hierarchically「階層的に」

Comprehension

本文の内容に合う文になるよう、最も適切な選択肢を1つ選びましょう。

1. College and university admissions requirements are _____ in Japan than they are in the US.
   a. easier
   b. painless
   c. more flexible
   d. stricter

2. Campus dorms are an important place to _____.
   a. socialize
   b. act formal
   c. attend class
   d. commute

3. According to the essay, some college students are employed to _____.
   a. pass the time
   b. gain necessary life experience
   c. fund their education
   d. earn spending money

4. According to the essay, underage drinking is _____.
   a. rare in most colleges
   b. common in most colleges
   c. a punishable offense
   d. an unpopular social activity

5. A major difference between Japanese and American culture is that _____.
   a. young people are much ruder in the US than in Japan
   b. politeness is unvalued in the US
   c. status is more important in Japan than in the US
   d. Americans are direct, while Japanese are indirect

Dialogue

次の会話の音声を聞いて、ペアで練習をしてみましょう。

Steve: Hey Yuko.
Yuko: Hi Steve. I haven't seen you for a while.
Steve: Yeah, I've been quite busy working on a term paper for my history class.
Yuko: I see.
Steve: I really like your sweater. Is it new?
Yuko: Thank you. Yes, my sister gave it to me.
Steve: Blue really suits you.
Yuko: Thanks a lot.
Steve: I need to get to the library, so I'll catch you later.
Yuko: See you later.

Listening Comprehension

音声を聞き、上のDialogueの内容に合う最も適切な選択肢を1つ選びましょう。

1. Steve and Yuko are _____.
   a.
   b.
   c.

2. Steve has been busy _____.
   a.
   b.
   c.

3. What is the most appropriate way to respond to a compliment?
   a.
   b.
   c.

Useful Expressions

次の日本文の意味になるように、適切なものを選んで英文を完成させましょう。

1. 日本の大学生は勉強ばかりでなくアルバイトもします。

    Japanese college students not only study _____.
    - a. yet have part-time jobs
    - b. but also have to part-time jobs
    - c. and have part-time jobs
    - d. but also hold part-time jobs

2. ハーゲンダッツのアイスクリームは、アメリカで始まりましたが、世界的に人気があります。

    Hägan-dazs ice cream _____ from the United States, but it enjoys world-wide popularity.
    - a. develops
    - b. original
    - c. originates
    - d. terminates

3. アメリカの大学生の多くは、授業以外の多くの活動をします。

    Many American college students are _____ in many extracurricular activities.
    - a. engages
    - b. engaged
    - c. committed
    - d. commits

4. 奨学金は、大学教育の大きな出費を賄います。

    The student's scholarship _____ the high costs of college education.
    - a. delays
    - b. increases
    - c. mediates
    - d. offsets

5. アメリカの学生達は、自由な時間がある時は寮の他の部屋に出かけて行きます。

    In their free time, college students in the US often _____ in the dorm.
    - a. spend
    - b. hang out
    - c. roam out
    - d. stay out

Discussion Topics

以下のトピックについて、グループで話し合ってみましょう。

1. Discuss the appealing and unappealing aspects of American college life.
2. Compare and contrast Japanese and American students' leisure time activities.
3. This unit discusses how Japanese and English compliments are different. What are the difficult parts of learning English for you?

Unit 2
Family Life

アメリカでは家庭観が現在大きく変わってきています。離婚と再婚が多くなり、片方の親だけの家庭、未婚の親の家庭、再婚により子供達が新しく兄弟になったり、子供達が父親と母親の家で交互に暮らす家庭も珍しくありません。また、皆を平等にして、相手の要求通りにすることがアメリカ人家庭のもてなし方であることにも注目してみましょう。

Vocabulary Quiz

次の語句の意味を a.～j. から選び、( ) 内に記号を記入しましょう。

1. traditional family　　　(　)　　a. もてなし
2. remarriage　　　　　　(　)　　b. 同棲
3. blended family　　　　(　)　　c. 不慣れな
4. cohabitation　　　　　(　)　　d. 不活発な
5. hospitality　　　　　　(　)　　e. 伝統的な家庭
6. proactive　　　　　　　(　)　　f. 優柔不断の
7. inactive　　　　　　　　(　)　　g. 混合家族
8. unaccustomed　　　　(　)　　h. 活発な
9. noncommittal response　(　)　　i. 再婚
10. indecisive　　　　　　(　)　　j. 気のない返事

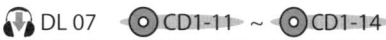

Reading

太字の語句に注意して、以下の英文を読みましょう。

1 Families in the United States are complex and diverse. **"Traditional" families** that consist of a stay-at-home mother, working father, and children are less common than they were in the past. Currently, dual-income households where both parents work outside the home and share domestic work are widespread and regarded as normal. At the same time, however, long-established norms continue to influence society, so both stay-at-home and working mothers tend to perform more housework and childcare than fathers.

2 In addition to dual-income households, "alternative" families are increasingly commonplace. A single-parent household can result from divorce, widowhood, or an unmarried person's desire to be a parent. Due to the high rate of divorce and remarriage, many children live with one parent part-time and frequently shuttle between two houses. If a parent **remarries**, children learn to live with their stepsiblings in a **"blended" family**. Furthermore, **cohabitation** is much more common in the United States than in Japan. Thus, some cohabiting couples never marry while others marry after several years of cohabitation.

3 Japanese students who do homestays will notice how the method of expressing **hospitality** varies in Japanese and American cultures. In the United States, people display hospitality through friendliness and treating others as equals. Therefore, most hostparents expect their homestay students to do many things independently, such as do their own laundry, prepare their own breakfast, and be **proactive** and independent versus **inactive** and dependent. In contrast, *omotenashi* defines hospitality in Japan, so hosts/hostesses and salesclerks treat their guests and customers as superiors. The expression "the customer is God" (*okyakusama wa kamisama desu*) captures Japanese *omotenashi*, and customers learn to expect excellent service. On the other hand, Americans are **unaccustomed** to assuming an inferior position in relation to others, so customers or guests are not usually treated with what Japanese consider respect. While Japanese may feel that American hospitality is cold or overly relaxed, Americans show hospitality through expressing friendliness and making others feel comfortable.

4 In American homes, guests are expected to explicitly express their needs and desires. If a guest is offered refreshments, the person should accept or decline without hesitation. Unlike in Japan, there is no expectation that the guest

exhibit restraint or utter a neutral response. A guest in America who declines the
initial offer may discover that the host/hostess never re-offers. **Noncommittal
responses** make the guest appear **indecisive** and unable to express individual
desire, and noncommittal people are regarded unfavorably in American culture.

Notes

dual-income household「共働きの家庭」 long-established norms「長期に確立された規範」
increasingly commonplace「次第に普通になっている」 widowhood「配偶者に先立たれたこと」 exhibit restraint「遠慮する」

Comprehension

本文の内容に合う文になるよう、最も適切な選択肢を1つ選びましょう。

1. Families in the US are _____.
   a. decreasing
   b. consistent
   c. similar
   d. dissimilar

2. A single-parent household can result from _____.
   a. income instability
   b. a spouse's death
   c. social pressure
   d. an irresponsible spouse

3. Americans show hospitality through _____.
   a. informality
   b. formality
   c. exhibiting reserve
   d. attentiveness

4. In the US, guests should express their feelings and desires _____.
   a. implicitly
   b. explicitly
   c. carefully
   d. carelessly

5. In the US, people who do not express their opinions are regarded _____.
   a. irrelevantly
   b. neutrally
   c. favorably
   d. unfavorably

▶ Dialogue

次の会話の音声を聞いて、ペアで練習をしてみましょう。

Anne: Hi Satoshi. Welcome to our home.
Satoshi: I'm so glad to be here.
Anne: Let's head into the living room. Please make yourself at home. You must be exhausted from your trip. Would you like something to drink?
Satoshi: That sounds great.
Anne: We have Coke, iced tea, milk, orange juice, or I could put on a pot of coffee. What are you in the mood for?
Satoshi: Anything is fine.
Anne: Why don't you come into the kitchen and choose your own drink?
Satoshi: Okay.
Anne: Here's a glass. Feel free to help yourself to anything in the refrigerator or pantry. My home is your home.
Satoshi: Thank you. I'm going to have a glass of iced tea.

▋ *Listening Comprehension*

音声を聞き、上のDialogueの内容に合う最も適切な選択肢を1つ選びましょう。

1. Satoshi is _____.
   a.
   b.
   c.

2. American hosts expect guests to _____.
   a.
   b.
   c.

3. Anne invites Satoshi to _____.
   a.
   b.
   c.

Unit 2 Family Life

Useful Expressions

次の日本文の意味になるように、適切なものを選んで英文を完成させましょう。

1. スマートフォンは、次第に普通のものになっています。

    Smartphones are _____.
    - a. increasingly commonplace
    - b. decreasingly commonplace
    - c. uncommon
    - d. no longer commonplace

2. 礼儀正しさの表し方は文化により異なります。

    The way that people _____ politeness varies by culture.
    - a. exerts
    - b. exert
    - c. displays
    - d. display

3. 日本文化では調和の維持が尊重されますので、自分の本当の感情や願望を表すことよりも、控えめにしなければなりません。

    Since Japanese culture attaches value to the maintenance of harmony, people must exhibit _____ rather than express their true feelings and desires.
    - a. restraint
    - b. freedom
    - c. careful
    - d. confidence

4. 勉強を怠る学生は、試験で良い成績を取ることが困難であることが分かることでしょう。

    A student who neglects his/her studies may _____ that it is difficult to perform well on the examination.
    - a. argue
    - b. discuss
    - c. discover
    - d. uncover

5. マイケル・ジャクソンは、「ポップミュージックの王様」と見なされています。

    Michael Jackson is _____ the "King of Pop" music.
    - a. regarded as
    - b. regarded for
    - c. known for
    - d. viewed

Discussion Topics

以下のトピックについて、グループで話し合ってみましょう。

1. Compare and contrast Japanese and American families.
2. What aspects of American hospitality would you find appealing or unappealing?
3. Do you think you would enjoy doing a homestay in the US? Explain your answer.

Unit 3

Food Culture

　アメリカでは、ニュー・イングランド地方のシーフードに代表される地方固有の食文化を除いては、日本ほどには食文化へのこだわりがないために、ファーストフードが早くから普及しました。近年では健康志向が強くなっていますが、共働きの夫婦が多く、外で食事をする機会が多くなっています。日米の食文化の違いに注目してみましょう。

 DL 10　 CD1-17

▶ Vocabulary Quiz

次の語句の意味を a. ～ j. から選び、( ) 内に記号を記入しましょう。

1.	local specialty	( )	**a.**	重要な
2.	stereotype	( )	**b.**	定額の
3.	balanced meals	( )	**c.**	お客
4.	crucial	( )	**d.**	自覚
5.	awareness	( )	**e.**	配列
6.	nutritious	( )	**f.**	地方の名物
7.	homemade meal	( )	**g.**	栄養の整った食事
8.	patron	( )	**h.**	典型
9.	array	( )	**i.**	家庭料理
10.	prix fixe	( )	**j.**	栄養のある

Reading

太字の語句に注意して、以下の英文を読みましょう。

[1] The United States has no distinct food culture. While specific places have local specialties, people do not eagerly anticipate tasting the **local specialty** when they travel. Food plays a much less significant role in American culture compared to Japanese culture.

[2] There is an inaccurate **stereotype** that the United States does not have regional cuisine, so Americans often only eat hot dogs, hamburgers, and other fast food items when they are away from home. However, the United States does indeed have regional specialties. For example, seafood is abundant in New England (Connecticut, Maine, Massachusetts, New Hampshire, Rhode Island, and Vermont). Fried food is very common in the Southeastern United States. In fact, the fast-food chain Kentucky Fried Chicken originated in the state of Kentucky. The Southwestern United States is famous for Tex-Mex food which combines the cuisine of Texas and Mexico and tends to be very spicy.

[3] Unfortunately, many Americans do not regard eating **balanced meals** as a **crucial** part of their daily lives. There is increasing **awareness** of the importance of healthy eating, but Americans spend little time cooking **nutritious homemade meals**. Instead, they buy prepared frozen meals, order pizza or other fast food, and eat many snacks and processed foods. In dual-income families, it is very difficult for spouses to spend time preparing meals on weeknights. Consequently, obesity and other health-related issues are major social problems in the United States.

[4] The experience of dining out in the United States is very different from eating out in Japan. As choice and individual freedom are prized in the United States, restaurants offer their **patrons** many choices. For instance, a customer orders a steak dinner, and the restaurant server asks the customer how he or she would like the meat cooked. The customer can choose rare, medium, or well-done. The dinner also comes with side dishes, so the customer can choose a vegetable and then a potato (mashed, French fries, or baked). Likewise, eggs can be prepared fried (sunny side up, over easy, or over hard), poached, or scrambled. Throughout the dining experience, the customer is presented with an **array** of choices. This style is very different from the Japanese style where one usually selects a set lunch or *omakase* course. There is an implicit assumption that the chef will prepare a delicious meal. During major holiday seasons, restaurants in the United States offer **prix fixe** (fixed price) meals which are similar to course meals in Japan.

play a role「役割を果たす」 inaccurate「不明確な」 cuisine「調理法」 prepared「出来合いの」 dual-income「夫婦ともが稼ぎ手」 obesity「肥満」 poached「ゆでた」 scrambled「混ぜながら焼いた」

Comprehension

本文の内容に合う文になるよう、最も適切な選択肢を1つ選びましょう。

1. Food is _____ in America than in Japan.
   a. very important
   b. less important
   c. neutral
   d. toxic

2. Regional specialties _____ in the US.
   a. reside
   b. exist
   c. are uncommon
   d. are overdeveloped

3. Many Americans are _____ about following a nutritious diet.
   a. interested
   b. unconcerned
   c. conscious
   d. concerned

4. At restaurants, Americans _____ choices over pre-selected meals.
   a. prefer
   b. dislike
   c. reject
   d. accept

5. At restaurants in Japan, the customer _____ the chef to prepare a delicious meal.
   a. facilitates
   b. enables
   c. distrusts
   d. trusts

Dialogue

次の会話の音声を聞いて、ペアで練習をしてみましょう。

Staff: Welcome to Subway. May I take your order?
Yuko: I would like a foot long roast beef sub on wheat.
Staff: What kind of cheese?
Yuko: What kinds do you have?
Staff: We have American, cheddar, or Swiss.
Yuko: Swiss.
Staff: What vegetables would you like on it?
Yuko: I'll take the works, but hold the hot peppers.
Staff: What type of sauce would you like on it?
Yuko: Light mayonnaise.
Staff: Would you like anything else?
Yuko: No, you can ring me up.

Listening Comprehension

音声を聞き、上のDialogueの内容に合う最も適切な選択肢を1つ選びましょう。

1. Yuko orders a submarine sandwich (sub) with _____.
   a. _____
   b. _____
   c. _____

2. Yuko wants to know _____.
   a. _____
   b. _____
   c. _____

3. Subway offers its patrons _____.
   a. _____
   b. _____
   c. _____

Useful Expressions

次の日本文の意味になるように、適切なものを選んで英文を完成させましょう。

1. 和食は日本文化で重要な役割を果たしていて、ユネスコの無形文化遺産に登録されています。

   Japanese cuisine _____ a significant role in Japanese culture and is on UNESCO's intangible cultural heritage list.

   a. functions   c. is
   b. sets   d. plays

2. クラムチャウダーは、ニュー・イングランド特有のものです。

   Clam chowder is a _____ in New England.

   a. transported   c. local specialty
   b. widespread   d. uncommon

3. 手先を使って食べるのは、インドでは普通のことです。

   Eating some foods with your hands is _____ India.

   a. rare   c. unknown in
   b. rude in   d. common in

4. ピザは、イタリアが発祥の地です。

   Pizza _____ Italy.

   a. is original   c. originates
   b. originated in   d. come from

5. 日本は、電子機器や自動車で有名です。

   Japan is _____ electronics and automobiles.

   a. famous for   c. familiar with
   b. famous with   d. full of

Discussion Topics

以下のトピックについて、グループで話し合ってみましょう。

1. Do you think young Japanese people are health conscious?
2. Do you prefer the American or Japanese style of restaurant dining?
3. Compare and contrast the advantages and disadvantages of a Japanese versus American diet.

Unit 4

Holidays

　アメリカの休日は宗教に由来するものとそうでないものがありますが、文化的に大きな意味を持っています。感謝祭は、北米の最初の清教徒達が豊かな収穫を神に感謝したことに由来しています。クリスマスは、プレゼント交換の他に教会で祈りを捧げた後、かしこまった食事をする日であることにも注意を向けてみましょう。

DL 14　CD1-24

Vocabulary Quiz

次の語句の意味を a.～j. から選び、（ ）内に記号を記入しましょう。

1. religious significance　（　）　　a. 楽しい
2. pilgrim　（　）　　b. クリスマス用の靴下
3. ample harvest　（　）　　c. 交換留学生
4. church service　（　）　　d. 巡礼者
5. joyful　（　）　　e. 最高潮に達する
6. memorialize　（　）　　f. 暖炉
7. Christmas stocking　（　）　　g. 豊かな収穫
8. fireplace　（　）　　h. 礼拝式
9. culminate　（　）　　i. 記念する
10. exchange student　（　）　　j. 宗教的意義

Reading

太字の語句に注意して、以下の英文を読みましょう。

1 Holidays have a long history in the United States and consequently are an important part of the culture. Many holidays have **religious significance,** but the traditions and customs are celebrated by both religious and non-religious people. While there are many holidays in the US, this unit focuses on Thanksgiving and Christmas.

2 Thanksgiving was first celebrated in the United States by a group of **pilgrims** and North American Indians. The pilgrims or "Puritans" designated Thanksgiving as a day to praise God for an **ample harvest** and surviving in a harsh new environment. Currently, people spend the day with family and eat foods such as turkey, stuffing, mashed potatoes with gravy, sweet potatoes, cranberry sauce, corn, fall vegetables, and pumpkin pie. Religious individuals may attend a **church service** on Thanksgiving Day.

3 The Christmas season is perhaps the most **joyful** period of the entire year. For Christians, this day **memorializes** Jesus Christ's birth. Christmas is thus a special day for Christians and many attend Church. Christmas songs which celebrate Christ's birth are an important part of the liturgy. For most people, the Christmas season is a time to exhibit generosity toward others. Most people buy and decorate a real or artificial evergreen tree with ornaments. On Christmas Eve, many people elect to go Christmas caroling and sing both religious and secular songs. In the home, children hang their **Christmas stockings** by the **fireplace** and leave out milk and cookies for Santa Clause. On Christmas morning, presents are under the tree and the Christmas stockings are filled with gifts. The day is spent exchanging presents and often **culminates** with a meal. Typical Christmas fare includes turkey or ham, vegetables, mashed potatoes, Christmas cookies, and various pies. On both Thanksgiving and Christmas, some people spend part of the day as volunteers to help the less fortunate.

4 Some people regard certain holidays as a precious time to spend with family. However, **exchange students** may be invited to someone's house on a holiday. Food is typically served family style, so individuals select the desired amount of food from large plates. To show hospitality, a host or hostess typically asks guests if they would like additional food or beverages and guests can freely accept or decline the offer.

Thanksgiving「感謝祭（アメリカでは11月第4木曜日）」 North American Indians「アメリカ・インディアン（北米大陸の先住民）」 Puritan「ピューリタン（清教徒）」 Jesus Christ「イエス・キリスト」 liturgy「礼拝式」 ornament「装飾」 secular「世俗的な」

Comprehension

本文の内容に合う文になるよう、最も適切な選択肢を1つ選びましょう。

1. Religious holidays are important _____.
   a. only to religious people
   b. in both religious and secular cultures
   c. because they are holidays
   d. to honor famous people

2. Thanksgiving started as a holiday to _____.
   a. thank God
   b. celebrate the Pilgrims' and North American Indians' friendship
   c. honor people who died in North America
   d. attend church

3. Christmas celebrates _____.
   a. children   c. Jesus Christ's birth
   b. the start of winter   d. Saint Nicholas's birth

4. During the Christmas season, people tend to be _____.
   a. depressed   c. greedy
   b. selfish   d. generous

5. Holidays are a time to spend with _____.
   a. strangers   c. friends
   b. a boyfriend or girlfriend   d. family

Dialogue

次の会話の音声を聞いて、ペアで練習をしてみましょう。

Yumiko: This meal was wonderful Jake. That was my first time to try meatloaf, and I really liked it.

Jake: I'm so glad. Meatloaf is an all-American classic. Would you like some more?

Yumiko: No thank you. I don't think that I could eat another bite.

Jake: I hope that you saved room for dessert because I made carrot cake.

Yumiko: That sounds really good, but I'm stuffed. I'm sorry.

Jake: There's no need to apologize. I want you to feel at home here, so feel free to eat and drink as much or as little as you want.

Yumiko: Thanks so much Jake. You're a great host.

Jake: My pleasure.

Listening Comprehension

音声を聞き、上のDialogueの内容に合う最も適切な選択肢を1つ選びましょう。

1. Yumiko _____ Jake's offer of more meatloaf.
   a.
   b.
   c.

2. Yumiko feels _____ .
   a.
   b.
   c.

3. Jake attempts to make Yumiko feel _____ .
   a.
   b.
   c.

Useful Expressions

次の日本文の意味になるように、適切なものを選んで英文を完成させましょう。

1. 合衆国政府は、マーティン・ルーサー・キング牧師の誕生日を連邦の祭日にしました。
   The United States government _____ Martin Luther King's birthday as a federal holiday.
   - **a.** demolished
   - **b.** created
   - **c.** abolished
   - **d.** designated

2. お盆休暇は、日本文化の中で特別な意味を持っています。
   The *Obon* Holiday has _____ significance in Japanese culture.
   - **a.** neutral
   - **b.** specialist
   - **c.** special
   - **d.** various

3. 学生は、宿題をするのに沢山の時間をかけました。
   The student _____ a lot of time on the homework assignment.
   - **a.** showed
   - **b.** spent
   - **c.** gave
   - **d.** had

4. ベトナム退役軍人記念碑は、ベトナム戦争で亡くなった軍人を記念しています。
   The Vietnam Veterans Memorial _____ the military troops who died in the Vietnam War.
   - **a.** ignores
   - **b.** dishonors
   - **c.** commemorated
   - **d.** memorializes

5. コンサートは、歌手がお辞儀をした時に最高潮に達しました。
   The concert _____ with the singer taking a bow.
   - **a.** terminated
   - **b.** commenced
   - **c.** culminated
   - **d.** culinary

Discussion Topics

以下のトピックについて、グループで話し合ってみましょう。

1. Compare and contrast how people spend Christmas in Japan and the US.
2. Which American holiday foods would you like to try? Why?
3. In homes, Americans offer their guests many choices. Discuss the positive and negative aspects of this style.

Unit 5

Individualism

　個人主義が徹底しているアメリカでは、協調性が求められる日本とは違い、子供達は自己を表現する教育を受けて、自分の意見を持つようになります。個人主義と結びついているのがプライバシーの尊重で、親でも子供部屋に無断で入ることをしません。18歳になると親から自立することが求められこ とに注目してみましょう。

 DL 18　 CD1-31

▶ Vocabulary Quiz

次の語句の意味を a. 〜 j. から選び、（ ）内に記号を記入しましょう。

1. obligation　　　　　（　　）　　a. 要約する
2. encapsulate　　　　（　　）　　b. 家事
3. self-expression　　　（　　）　　c. 個人の空間
4. inability　　　　　　（　　）　　d. 私生活
5. articulate　　　　　（　　）　　e. 自立した
6. privacy　　　　　　（　　）　　f. 義務
7. personal space　　　（　　）　　g. 推移
8. self-reliant　　　　　（　　）　　h. 無力
9. housework　　　　　（　　）　　i. 自己表現
10. transition　　　　　（　　）　　j. はっきり述べる

Reading

太字の語句に注意して、以下の英文を読みましょう。

1　The United States is a country of immigrants. The original settlers left their homeland in England to pursue a new life in North America and later achieved independence from England and the area they settled became the United States of America. Individualism is such a cherished value in the United States that the US is regarded as one of the most individualistic countries in the world. As a result, Americans seem to make decisions without feelings of duty or **obligation** to others.

2　Two proverbs illustrate how individuality is valued in the United States and conformity is prized in Japan. "The nail that sticks up gets hammered down" (*deru kui wa utareru*) reflects the admiration of conformity in Japan. On the other hand, "the squeaky wheel gets the grease" **encapsulates** the importance of individuality and nonconformity in the United States. From a young age, Americans learn the importance of forming and expressing an opinion. Elementary schools require that young children participate in show and tell sessions. During these sessions, each student stands in front of the class and presents an item such as a favorite stuffed animal. The student speaks about the item to members of the class. As individuals in the US learn the art of **self-expression** from a very young age, they view those with the **inability** to **articulate** their opinions, preferences, and feelings negatively.

3　Closely connected to individualism, **privacy** is valued in US culture. Many children have their own bedrooms that they regard as their **personal space**. A bedroom is the place where people can relax and spend time alone. Parents typically refrain from entering the room without the child's permission in order to respect the child's privacy. In general, Americans frequently express their desire to spend some personal time alone each day either in their bedrooms or elsewhere.

4　As individuality and independence are interrelated, individuals are expected to be **self-reliant**. For example, many Japanese college students continue to live with their parents and commute to college. Living at home is easier than living independently because most mothers take care of the **housework** and cooking. In contrast, American teenagers want to leave home once they turn eighteen. Many young people view moving out of their parents' home as a crucial step toward achieving independence and **transitioning** into adulthood. While the global economic crisis of the 2000s has prevented many young people from leaving their parents' homes, their preference is to move out of their parents' homes and either share an apartment with roommates or live alone.

Notes

settler「開拓移民」 homeland「故郷」 individualism「個人主義」 cherish「大切にする」 proverb「ことわざ」 conformity「画一性」 squeaky「キーキーときしむ」 interrelated「相関した」 commute「通う」

Comprehension

本文の内容に合う文になるよう、最も適切な選択肢を1つ選びましょう。

1. The US population is composed of _____.
   a. people from other countries
   b. a uniform population
   c. a decreasing number of people
   d. an increasing number of people

2. American culture values _____.
   a. obedience
   b. neutrality
   c. uniqueness
   d. conformity

3. In the US, the ability to express oneself is _____.
   a. avoided
   b. uncommon
   c. unimportant
   d. crucial

4. Most Americans regard privacy and personal space as _____.
   a. irrelevant
   b. ordinary
   c. voluntary
   d. vital

5. In the US, the ability to live independently signals _____.
   a. maturity
   b. immaturity
   c. dependence
   d. family

🎧 DL 20 💿 CD1-36

Dialogue

次の会話の音声を聞いて、ペアで練習をしてみましょう。

Jennifer: So how's your homestay going?

Kenji: Pretty good, but I have noticed some cultural differences. Since my host mother has a full-time job, I often come home to an empty house.

Jennifer: I can understand how that must feel strange, but this situation is common.

Kenji: I see. It's also difficult for me to get used to making my own plans each weekend.

Jennifer: How so?

Kenji: In Japan, a host family would definitely show the foreign student around the area. My host mother showed me around one weekend, but now she expects me to plan my own weekends.

Jennifer: Your homestay is typical. Most American people value independence. Many American teenagers would love to have complete freedom on the weekends.

Kenji: American teenagers are quite different from Japanese teens.

Jennifer: There are definitely a lot of adjustments to make when you're living with a family in a foreign culture. Let me know if you want to hang out some weekend.

Kenji: Thanks. That would be great.

■ *Listening Comprehension*   🎧 DL 21 💿 CD1-37

音声を聞き、上のDialogueの内容に合う最も適切な選択肢を1つ選びましょう。

1. Kenji feels _____ in his current homestay situation.
   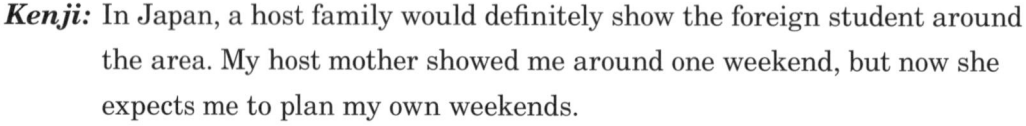
   a.
   b.
   c.

2. Kenji is _____ to making plans each weekend.
   a.
   b.
   c.

24

Useful Expressions

次の日本文の意味になるように、適切なものを選んで英文を完成させましょう。

1. アメリカ合衆国は、才能のある人で成り立つ国です。

    The United States is a country _____.
    - a. over talented people
    - b. of talented people
    - c. where talented people
    - d. in trouble

2. その学生は、英語を勉強するためにカリフォルニアで春休みを過ごしました。

    The student spent spring vacation in California to _____.
    - a. the study of English
    - b. hang out the study of English
    - c. pursue the study of English
    - d. follow the study of English

3. 学生達は、競技会に参加しました。

    The students _____ the athletic competition.
    - a. participated in
    - b. presided over
    - c. refused
    - d. involved

4. 彼は、交渉術を全く身に付けませんでした。

    He never learned the art of _____.
    - a. ignorance
    - b. profit
    - c. negotiation
    - d. galleries

5. この建物の中では喫煙は控えなければなりません。

    People should _____ from smoking inside the building.
    - a. avoid
    - b. prohibit
    - c. refrain
    - d. refuse

Discussion Topics

以下のトピックについて、グループで話し合ってみましょう。

1. Do you think that Japanese are becoming more individualistic? Explain your opinion.
2. Do you think that people are still pressured to conform to the group in Japan? Explain your opinion.
3. Do you think that Japanese people should learn to be more independent? Explain your opinion.

Unit 6

Socializing at Parties

　　パーティーは、アメリカの社会生活の中で重要な役割を果たしています。家やプールサイドでのパーティー、学校でのダンス・パーティー、その他様々な種類のパーティーがあります。パーティーではアルコールが飲まれますが、日本とは違い先輩・後輩の区別はなく、知らない人との会話が頻繁に行われます。アメリカでのパーティーの役割に注目してみましょう。

DL 22　　CD1-38

Vocabulary Quiz

次の語句の意味を a. ~ j. から選び、( ) 内に記号を記入しましょう。

1. social scene　　　　　(　)　　a. 酔った
2. alcohol consumption　(　)　　b. 食事持ち寄りパーティー
3. integral component　 (　)　　c. 軽飲食物
4. residence　　　　　　(　)　　d. 自発的な
5. refreshments　　　　 (　)　　e. 団結
6. potluck party　　　　 (　)　　f. 社会風景
7. venue　　　　　　　　(　)　　g. 住宅
8. spontaneous　　　　 (　)　　h. 不可欠な要素
9. solidarity　　　　　　(　)　　i. 酒類の消費
10. drunk　　　　　　　　(　)　　j. 場所

Reading

太字の語句に注意して、以下の英文を読みましょう。

1　Parties are a central element of the US **social scene**. **Alcohol consumption** and informal partying are **integral components** of American culture. Other types of parties include birthday, cocktail, dinner, and special occasion parties or "celebrations" (for example, St. Patrick's Day and the Super Bowl).

2　House parties and pool parties are popular among teenagers and young adults. House parties occur at private **residences** and the host/hostess serves a variety of **refreshments** to the attendees. Guests relax at the host/hostess's home by conversing, listening to music, and dancing. As the name implies, pool parties take place around swimming pools and an assortment of food and beverages is served. At **potluck parties**, the host or hostess asks guests to bring food or beverages in order to absorb some of the costs.

3　School dances are another popular type of party. Most famously, the high school prom is a semi-formal event that is held during the junior or senior year of high school. Typically, couples meet at someone's house to take single or group photographs, and then use a car or limousine as transportation to the prom **venue**. Students engage in dancing throughout the evening and elect a prom king and queen. Post-prom parties or events usually follow the prom and occur at a restaurant, entertainment venue, or a student's home.

4　Socialization in Japan typically involves going out or talking with friends and acquaintants, while people in the US actively pursue meeting new people at a party. Consequently, the ability to make impromptu conversation with strangers or acquaintances is a necessary skill in the US. Small talk is **spontaneous** talk about topics such as music, sports, television and movies, and the weather. Such talk enables people to form bonds and build **solidarity** with others. While there is a tendency to exchange opinions and debate in American culture, the purpose of small talk in Japanese is oriented toward building solidarity and establishing interpersonal connections.

5　One can also observe a difference in etiquette at American parties and Japanese *nomikai*. As the US prizes individualism, there is little pressure to drink alcohol. Non-drinkers can easily express their preference for nonalcoholic beverages. Another notable difference between the US and Japan is that there is no custom for a *kohai* to pour alcohol for his or her *senpai* in the US. In fact, the *senpai-kohai* distinction is nonexistent in American culture. Although students may become **drunk** at parties or bars, it is considered socially unacceptable for adults to become publicly intoxicated in the US.

Notes

St. Patrick's Day「聖パトリックの日（3月17日）」（アイルランドにキリスト教を広めた聖パトリックの命日に由来する。聖パトリックがキリスト教の三位一体の教義を説明するために緑のクローバーの葉を使ったと言われていることから、この日には緑の色が尊重される。アイルランド系の移民の多いニューヨークなどの都市でパレードが行われる。）　Super Bowl「スーパー・ボウル」（アメリカン・フットボールの年間チャンピオンを決める試合。テレビの視聴率は45パーセントを越えることが多い。）　attendee「出席者」　converse「会話する」　assortment「詰め合わせ」　prom「（promenadeの短縮形）高校や大学の卒業記念のダンス・パーティー」　socialization「交流」　acquaintance「知り合い」　impromptu conversation「即座の会話」　interpersonal connections「人間相互の結びつき」　publicly intoxicated「公衆の前で酔っぱらった」

Comprehension

本文の内容に合う文になるよう、最も適切な選択肢を1つ選びましょう。

1. In the US, parties are _____.
   a. popular
   b. unpopular
   c. decreasing
   d. increasing

2. At parties, people in the US _____.
   a. only talk to old acquaintances
   b. meet new people
   c. pour drinks for others
   d. leave early

3. Small talk is _____.
   a. discussing important matters
   b. a form of networking
   c. common at parties
   d. rare at parties, but common in the home

4. In the US, people _____.
   a. are pressured to drink alcohol
   b. are not pressured to drink alcohol
   c. pour drinks for each other
   d. decline alcoholic beverages

5. In the US, public drunkenness is _____.
   a. acceptable
   b. taboo
   c. common
   d. necessary

Dialogue

次の会話の音声を聞いて、ペアで練習をしてみましょう。

Dan: Hi I'm Dan. It's nice to meet you.
Yui: I'm Yui. Nice to meet you too.
Dan: So what's your major?
Yui: English literature. I'm an exchange student from Japan.
Dan: That's cool. How long will you be staying in the US?
Yui: About a year.
Dan: I've never been to Japan, but I think Japanese animation is totally cool.
Yui: I'm glad to hear that.
Dan: Yeah, Hayao Miyazaki is a genius.
Yui: *Princess Mononoke* is my favorite film.
Dan: I never saw that one, but I loved *Spirited Away*.
Yui: That's also a great movie.
Dan: I need to go and talk to some other people. It was great talking with you.
Yui: I enjoyed meeting you too. Hope to see you around campus.

Listening Comprehension

音声を聞き、上のDialogueの内容に合う最も適切な選択肢を1つ選びましょう。

1. Yui and Dan are _____.
   a.
   b.
   c.

2. Dan _____.
   a.
   b.
   c.

3. Dan ends the conversation with Yui because he _____.
   a.
   b.
   c.

Useful Expressions

次の日本文の意味になるように、適切なものを選んで英文を完成させましょう。

1. 携帯電話は、日本の若者文化を構成する不可欠の要素です。

    Mobile phones are an _____ component of Japanese youth culture.
    - a. integral
    - b. central
    - c. nonessential
    - d. integrate

2. お客全てがパーティーの費用を軽減するのに役立つようにパーティーの主催者にお金をあげました。

    Every guest gave the party host money to help _____ the costs of the party.
    - a. absorb
    - b. improve
    - c. swallow
    - d. accept

3. 交際の多くは、日本式のバーで始まります。

    Much socialization _____ at Japanese style bars.
    - a. participates
    - b. involves
    - c. occurs
    - d. endures

4. 反対意見を直接的に表現することは、日本では受け入れ難いことです。

    Expressing direct disagreement is considered _____ in Japan.
    - a. acceptable
    - b. unacceptable
    - c. relevant
    - d. often

5. カレンはサッカーの練習に参加していなかったのですが、先週キャンパスで私は彼女と偶然出会いました。

    Karen has not been attending soccer practice, but I _____ campus last week.
    - a. bumped her on
    - b. meet her in
    - c. saw her over
    - d. saw her around

Discussion Topics

以下のトピックについて、グループで話し合ってみましょう。

1. Compare and contrast Japanese and American parties.
2. Which type of American parties would you find appealing or unappealing? Explain your answer.
3. Do you think you would enjoy socializing in the US? Explain your answer.

Unit 7

Dating and Romance

　　デートは、若者にとっての関心事です。アメリカでは社会生活の上で重要な要素になっていて、様々な問題の原因にもなっています。結婚前の性的関係が多い反面、女性には社会的に厳しい視線が注がれる傾向もあります。職場結婚が少ないアメリカで、デートがどのような役割を果たしているかに注目してみましょう。

Vocabulary Quiz

次の語句の意味を a.～j. から選び、（ ）内に記号を記入しましょう。

1. adolescent （　　）　　a. お見合い結婚
2. undermine （　　）　　b. 運動競技
3. favorably （　　）　　c. 青春の
4. pregnancy （　　）　　d. 職場
5. sexually-transmitted disease （　　）　　e. 住む
6. arranged marriage （　　）　　f. 好意的に
7. reside （　　）　　g. 妊娠
8. athletics （　　）　　h. 性感染病
9. workplace （　　）　　i. 趣味
10. hobby （　　）　　j. 傷つける

Reading

太字の語句に注意して、以下の英文を読みましょう。

1 Dating is a central component of **adolescent** social life. Popular dating activities include having dinner and a movie, meeting for coffee, and engaging in a sport or leisure activity. Americans are typically involved in several romantic relationships over the course of their high school and college careers. Relationships range from more casual to serious. "Going out" is the term a couple uses to indicate that they are in a more serious, committed relationship.

2 American culture is quite tolerant of non-marital sexual intercourse. Many college-aged students engage in hookups; that is, short-term encounters. Some people even argue that the "hookup culture" is significantly **undermining** formal courtship or a "dating culture." Unfortunately, American culture views men who have multiple sexual partners much more approvingly than women with multiple partners. This phenomenon is referred to as a "sexual double standard" because women are regarded unfavorably and men **favorably** for engaging in the same behavior. Finally, the decision to become sexually active involves the risks of **pregnancy** and contracting a **sexually-transmitted disease (STD)**.

3 The dating culture in Japan is much weaker than that of the US. In the US, it is very common to bring a date to various social events or recreational activities, but couples often socialize separately in Japan. **Arranged marriages** were once commonplace in Japan, but love marriages have overwhelmingly replaced them. College life in the US provides students with more opportunities to meet a romantic partner than in Japan. As more students in the US **reside** on-campus or off-campus with other friends, there are many opportunities to socialize with other college students. Students also meet their partners through participation in clubs, organizations, and **athletics** or at bars or nightclubs.

4 Similar to in Japan, some people meet their partner or future husband or wife at the **workplace**, but this pattern is more prevalent in Japan than it is in the US. As there is a tendency to separate personal and professional life in American culture, more opportunities exist outside the workplace to meet a romantic partner such as through membership in an organization or church, the pursuit of a **hobby** or sport, and social events organized for singles. Although online dating has many drawbacks, this is another way to meet a romantic partner.

Notes

tolerant「寛容な」 non-marital「未婚の」 sexual intercourse「性交渉」 courtship「求愛」 sexual double standard「性に関する二重基準」 recreational activities「娯楽活動」 commonplace「普通の」 overwhelmingly「圧倒的に」 socialize「交際する」 prevalent「普及している」 drawback「欠点」

Comprehension

本文の内容に合う文になるよう、最も適切な選択肢を 1 つ選びましょう。

1. "Going out" means that a couple is in a _____ relationship.
    a. casual
    b. serious
    c. new
    d. arranged

2. A "hookup" is a _____ relationship.
    a. definite
    b. brief
    c. long-term
    d. committed

3. According to the sexual double standard, _____.
    a. neither men nor women are evaluated
    b. men are viewed unfavorably
    c. women are viewed unfavorably
    d. men and women are viewed equally

4. The Japanese dating culture is weaker than the American one because _____.
    a. single-sex socialization is more common
    b. love marriages are on the rise
    c. college students reside off-campus
    d. all of the above

5. Workplace-generated love relationships are _____.
    a. more common in the US
    b. more common in Japan
    c. uncommon in both countries
    d. common in both counties

Dialogue

次の会話の音声を聞いて、ペアで練習をしてみましょう。

Nancy: I'm pretty psyched because I have a date this weekend.

Kentaro: That's great. So how do couples usually meet in the US?

Nancy: That depends. People meet around campus or off campus at a bar. Sometimes a person goes on a date with someone that he or she has never met. This is called a blind date. The way it works is a mutual acquaintance of both participants arranges the date.

Kentaro: That sounds like a Japanese "gokon" or group blind date.

Nancy: How does it work?

Kentaro: Two single friends or acquaintances arrange the group date by bringing three or four of their own friends. The entire group meets at a Japanese-style bar, and the participants converse with each other. If two people hit it off, they might arrange an individual date.

Nancy: That's very different than dating in the US. I guess going out on a group date involves less pressure than an individual blind date.

Kentaro: It does. It was very nice talking with you, but I need to get to my next class.

Nancy: Okay. I'll see you later.

Listening Comprehension

音声を聞き、上のDialogueの内容に合う最も適切な選択肢を1つ選びましょう。

1. In the US, couples often meet _____.

    a.
    b.
    c.

2. People who go out on a blind date are _____.

    a.
    b.
    c.

Useful Expressions

次の日本文の意味になるように、適切なものを選んで英文を完成させましょう。

1. 日本の学生は大抵スポーツやクラブ活動に関わっています。

    Japanese students are usually _____ in sports or club activities.
    - a. involved
    - b. uninvolved
    - c. busy
    - d. participate

2. アメリカ文化は、多様性や異なった信条に寛容です。

    American culture is _____ of diversity and different beliefs.
    - a. acknowledge
    - b. intolerant
    - c. tolerant
    - d. accept

3. 父親はいつも息子の立場を支持しますが、そのことは彼の妻の権威を傷つけます。

    The father always supports his son's position, which _____ his wife's authority.
    - a. encourages
    - b. undermines
    - c. uncovers
    - d. support

4. ユミコは、外国に1年間住んだ後でようやくボーイフレンドに会えるのでわくわくしています。

    Yumiko is _____ because she will finally see her boyfriend after living abroad for a year.
    - a. unexcited
    - b. disappointed
    - c. psyched
    - d. disturbed

5. レイチェルとダンはパーティーで会って、すぐに相愛関係になりました。

    Rachel met Dan at a party and they immediately _____.
    - a. hit it off
    - b. hit it on
    - c. liked
    - d. suitable

Discussion Topics

以下のトピックについて、グループで話し合ってみましょう。

1. Discuss the most popular dating spots in Japan.
2. This unit discusses how Americans engage in many casual relationships. Do you think that dating is viewed more seriously in Japan than in the US?
3. Discuss the appealing and unappealing aspects of dating in the US.

Unit 8

Pluralistic Society

　北米大陸には先住民族がいましたが、そこにイギリス系やドイツ系をはじめとした多くの民族が移住してきたため、アメリカ文化は多元的になりました。様々な文化的特徴が別個に存続し、文化的偏見がありましたが、共通の価値観と共に民族的な「平等」が広く受容されています。一元的な日本文化との違いに注目してみましょう。

DL 30　CD1-53

Vocabulary Quiz

次の語句の意味を a.～j. から選び、( ) 内に記号を記入しましょう。

1. settler　　　　　（　）　　**a**. 多様な
2. descent　　　　（　）　　**b**. 排除
3. diverse　　　　 （　）　　**c**. 性差上の特質
4. distinguished 　（　）　　**d**. 寛容さ
5. legislation　　　（　）　　**e**. 開拓移民
6. tolerance　　　 （　）　　**f**. 普及した
7. pervasive　　　（　）　　**g**. 立法
8. sexuality　　　 （　）　　**h**. 包含
9. exclusion　　　（　）　　**i**. 家系
10. inclusion　　　（　）　　**j**. 顕著な

Reading

太字の語句に注意して、以下の英文を読みましょう。

1　The United States is a multicultural or pluralistic society. North American Indians or "Native Americans" were the original inhabitants of North America. The United States eventually became a colony of England, so English **settlers** immigrated to North America. As people of German, French, and Scots-Irish **descent** immigrated to the US, it gradually became known as a "nation of immigrants."

2　The metaphors of "melting pot" or "mosaic" are frequently applied to the US to indicate the **diverse** and heterogeneous nature of the society. Immigrants internalize many dominant American values, customs, and norms and thus experience a certain amount of cultural assimilation. At the same time, however, they maintain their own unique cultural customs and traditions. Many major cities such as Boston, New York, and San Francisco have a Chinatown as well as Italian or Hispanic sections that preserve these groups' distinct cultural heritages. Today, the US population consists of African-American/Black, Asian, Caucasian/White, Hispanic/Latino, Native American, and Native Hawaiian people in addition to biracial and multiracial individuals.

3　Since equality is a salient American cultural value, the US has a long and **distinguished** history of respecting cultural, ethnic, and religious differences and therein embracing diversity. In the past, US society was plagued by prejudice as well as racial and gender discrimination; however, the combined effects of **legislation**, education, and the resulting increased **tolerance** have cured these social illnesses to a large degree. While prejudice and discrimination still exist, women and minorities have made great advances in the journey toward greater social equality.

4　The demarcation between *uchi/soto* (in-group and out-group) is **pervasive** in Japanese culture. The fact that Japan is a relatively racially homogenous society is a potential explanation for the resilience of the *uchi/soto* distinction. The US, by contrast, makes no firm division between in and out groups. Individuals tend to form groups based on shared social categories such as age, race/ethnicity, gender, and **sexuality** but group membership is much more fluid than in Japan. Nevertheless, adolescents tend to form social cliques which are organized around **exclusion** and **inclusion** and thus similar to *uchi* and *soto*.

Notes

multicultural「多文化的な」 pluralistic「多元的な」 North American Indians「北米インディアン（クリストファー・コロンブス一行が北米大陸をインドだと勘違いしたことによる）」 heterogeneous「異質の」 internalize「吸収する」 cultural assimilation「文化的同化」 biracial「2民族の」 salient「顕著な」 therein「その中で」 demarcation「区別」 homogenous「同質性の」 resilience「活力」 social clique「社会上の派閥」

Comprehension

本文の内容に合う文になるよう、最も適切な選択肢を1つ選びましょう。

1. The United States can be characterized as a _____ society.
   - a. nationalistic
   - b. intolerant
   - c. heterogeneous
   - d. homogenous

2. In the US, immigrants _____.
   - a. only maintain their home culture
   - b. abandon their home culture
   - c. only internalize dominant culture values
   - d. both assimilate and maintain unique cultural customs

3. US culture highly values _____.
   - a. group identification
   - b. unfairness
   - c. equality
   - d. inequality

4. In the US, the distinction between in-group and out-group is _____.
   - a. more important than in Japan
   - b. less important than in Japan
   - c. nonexistent
   - d. frequent

5. For American adolescents, group identification _____.
   - a. increases one's popularity
   - b. decreases one's popularity
   - c. is unimportant
   - d. is important

Dialogue

次の会話の音声を聞いて、ペアで練習をしてみましょう。

Liz: How's your life in the US going?

Yuki: Pretty good, but I find it difficult to make friends in the US.

Liz: How so?

Yuki: I don't know how to form real friendships with them.

Liz: I see. International students sometimes criticize Americans because they are friendly and personable, yet they are difficult to form genuine friendships with.

Yuki: Just the other day someone said "we should grab coffee together sometime."

Liz: That's a great example. When a person says "sometime," the invitation is superficial, and you should not expect the person to reach out and contact you. They are just being polite.

Yuki: I didn't realize that. What do you suggest that I do?

Liz: Don't give up. I know that Japanese tend to be shy, but you need to be proactive by taking the initiative and asking someone to hang out.

Yuki: Taking the initiative is difficult.

Liz: I understand. Well, if you join a student organization or intramural sports team, then you will have additional socialization opportunities.

Yuki: That sounds like a good idea. I think I'll try that. Thanks for the tip.

Liz: Don't mention it.

Listening Comprehension

音声を聞き、上のDialogueの内容に合う最も適切な選択肢を1つ選びましょう。

1. Yuki finds making friends in the US _____.
   a.
   b.
   c.

2. Liz advises Yuki to be _____.
   a.
   b.
   c.

Useful Expressions

次の日本文の意味になるように、適切なものを選んで英文を完成させましょう。

1. 交換留学生は、チップを払うアメリカの習慣を身につけました。

    The exchange student has _____ the American custom of paying tips.

    a. externalized   c. attained

    b. internalized   d. achieved

2. 日本の夏は、台風や豪雨に悩まされます。

    In the summer, Japan is _____ typhoons and torrential rain.

    a. plagued by   c. resistant

    b. unaffected by   d. unsusceptible

3. 政治家は、社会的な病理を直すことを約束しました。

    The politician promised to _____ the social ills.

    a. cure   c. medicate

    b. recover   d. treatment

4. アメリカの中西部では竜巻がよく起こります。

    Tornados are _____ in the Midwestern US.

    a. pervade   c. pervasive

    b. throughout   d. infrequent

5. 彼女は、文章力向上の助けとなるヒントを私に与えてくれました。

    She gave me some _____ to help improve my writing.

    a. discouragement   c. tips

    b. news   d. proposals

Discussion Topics

以下のトピックについて、グループで話し合ってみましょう。

1. This unit discusses how the US is a mosaic of different cultures. Discuss the challenges of living in a pluralistic society.
2. The number of foreign residents in Japan is increasing. Discuss the potential effects of this phenomenon on Japanese culture.
3. This unit discusses how one must be proactive to form friendships with Americans. Would this be difficult for you? Explain.

Unit 9

Degree of Formality

　アメリカ文化は形式にとらわれないことが特徴で、ファーストネームで呼び合ったり、服装もカジュアルであったりしますが、これは文化的平等主義と結びついていて、社会的なタブーもほとんどありません。成人式のように横並びの習慣の多い日本の文化とは異なり、アメリカ文化では決まりが求められないことに注目してみましょう。

DL 34　CD2-01

Vocabulary Quiz

次の語句の意味を a. 〜 j. から選び、( ) 内に記号を記入しましょう。

1. prevalence　　　　　　　(　)　　**a.** 年金
2. consumption　　　　　　(　)　　**b.** 公共交通機関
3. strict　　　　　　　　　(　)　　**c.** 雇用
4. forbid　　　　　　　　　(　)　　**d.** 心付け
5. public transportation　　(　)　　**e.** 強制的退職年齢
6. employment　　　　　　(　)　　**f.** 厳密な
7. mandatory retirement age　(　)　**g.** 普及
8. pension　　　　　　　　(　)　　**h.** ふれ合う
9. gratuity　　　　　　　　(　)　　**i.** 飲食
10. interact　　　　　　　　(　)　　**j.** 禁止する

Reading

太字の語句に注意して、以下の英文を読みましょう。

[1]　In many ways, the US is an extremely informal culture. Informality is readily apparent in the custom of addressing others by first names, a casual style of dress, and manner of speaking. The pervasiveness of informality in American culture is interrelated to the cultural value of egalitarianism; that is, the US is not a very status-oriented culture.

[2]　To illustrate the **prevalence** of informality in US culture, there is no social taboo against the **consumption** of food and beverages in a wide array of public places. Students are often permitted to eat and drink in class, and teachers can be observed drinking and occasionally eating while teaching class. As **strict** rules that **forbid** eating and drinking on **public transportation** are nonexistent, people can be seen eating and drinking on buses, trains, and the subway.

[3]　Informality is also evident by the fact that American culture does not designate a certain time period when lifetime rites of passage should occur such as first **employment**, marriage, childbirth, and retirement. It is extremely common for college students to change majors several times prior to graduation. Similarly, employees work for several organizations or even change careers over the course of their professional lives. Colleges and universities enroll a diverse population from new high school graduates to middle-aged people who are undergoing career retraining. In addition, marriage and childbirth are not viewed as universal life milestones. Therefore, some couples never marry while others choose to marry and remain childless for various reasons, so-called "D.I.N.K.S." (Dual Income, No Kids). Certain professions such as airline pilots and military personnel impose a **mandatory retirement age**, but this practice is not universal. Consequently, employees retire at various ages. While some people become reemployed after retirement, many Americans with an adequate **pension** or financial resources take early retirement (e.g., 50s) and then pursue their personal hobbies or interests.

[4]　Many Japanese experience culture shock from the informal nature of American customer service. Restaurant wait staff or "servers" frequently address customers in a friendly, informal manner. The purpose of such informality is to create rapport with the customer. Most Americans are comfortable with this communication style, and the server's ability to build solidarity with customers can result in earning a larger **gratuity**. Similarly, staff members at many retail stores **interact** with their customers in an informal manner. Unfortunately, some

workers abuse the custom of informality and can be observed chatting with their colleagues during their work shifts.

[5] Informality and formality are also evident in language. The custom of using the appropriate honorifics in Japanese reflects formality, while the absence of a complex honorific system in American English shows informality. In contrast to Japanese, American English does not designate certain linguistic forms that one must use according to age and social status.

Notes

pervasiveness「広がり」 egalitarianism「平等主義」 status-oriented「地位志向の」 taboo「タブー（禁忌）」 beverage「飲み物」 rite of passage「通過儀礼」 childbirth「出産」 enroll「登録する」 retraining「再訓練」 rapport「関係」 honorific「敬語（の）」

Comprehension

本文の内容に合う文になるよう、最も適切な選択肢を1つ選びましょう。

1. The United States can be regarded as _____ society.
   a. a hierarchical   c. a status-oriented
   b. an egalitarian   d. a transitioning

2. The US is a _____ society than Japan.
   a. more formal   c. less democratic
   b. more informal   d. none of the above

3. The US _____ specific time periods for transitional life events.
   a. defines   c. maintains
   b. does not specify   d. characterizes

4. In the US, restaurant servers act informally in order to _____.
   a. earn a larger tip
   b. please their superiors c. feel comfortable
   d. indicate their dissatisfaction with the job

5. An honorific system _____ in American English.
   a. is developing   c. is nonexistent
   b. occurs   d. exists

Dialogue

次の会話の音声を聞いて、ペアで練習をしてみましょう。

Rei: So how do students find jobs in the US?

Carrie: Well, that depends. The job market is quite bleak right now. Students look for jobs in different ways. The internet, recruitment firms, and jobs fairs are all popular tools to search for jobs. How about in Japan?

Rei: Students begin job hunting during their junior or senior year. They wear dark-colored recruit suits and attend different companies' presentations and recruitment fairs. They also go through interviews and various tests at different companies. Successful applicants receive a *naitei* or provisional employment offer.

Carrie: That's quite different from the US. Job seekers in the US have to expend a lot of individual effort. Even students who use a recruiter also search for jobs themselves.

Rei: A student's university organizes many of the job-hunting events.

Carrie: These different job-hunting strategies show how self-reliance is pervasive in many areas of American life.

Rei: I agree. Japanese people prefer to follow a predetermined course.

Listening Comprehension

音声を聞き、上のDialogueの内容に合う最も適切な選択肢を1つ選びましょう。

1. In Japan, the job-hunting period is _____.

    a. _____
    b. _____
    c. _____

2. American culture values: _____.

    a. _____
    b. _____
    c. _____

Useful Expressions

次の日本文の意味になるように、適切なものを選んで英文を完成させましょう。

1. 日本車の品質の高さは、日本で正確さが普及していることの例となっています。

    The high quality of Japanese cars illustrates the _____ of precision in Japan.
    - a. rare
    - b. rareness
    - c. pervasive
    - d. pervasiveness

2. その学生が勉強家であることは、学業成績によって明らかになっています。

    The student's hard work is _____ by her academic achievements.
    - a. evident
    - b. evidence
    - c. show
    - d. attained

3. 彼女は、英会話の学校に入学しました。

    She _____ in an English conversation school.
    - a. success
    - b. enrolled
    - c. graduated
    - d. entered

4. 彼は、外向的な人で、様々な人との交流を楽しんでいます。

    He is an outgoing person and enjoys _____ various people.
    - a. resisting
    - b. escaping from
    - c. interacting with
    - d. avoiding

5. 彼女は、大学院にはいるために大変努力しました。

    She _____ a lot of effort to gain admission to graduate school.
    - a. expended
    - b. paid
    - c. produced
    - d. product

Discussion Topics

以下のトピックについて、グループで話し合ってみましょう。

1. This unit discusses how the US is an informal culture. Discuss the appealing and unappealing aspects of this cultural practice.
2. Why do you think that formality is so important in Japan?
3. The honorific system and *senpai-kohai* relations ensure that people express the appropriate amount of respect to others. Discuss the positive and negative aspects of these cultural practices.

Unit 10

Volunteerism

アメリカ文化では、ボランティア活動が尊重され、そのために個人の時間や技能が使われ、金銭が慈善組織に寄付されています。寄付金を集めるためのダンス、地域社会への文化貢献、外国で教育や農業の支援者として働くものまで様々です。ボランティア活動が文化の相互理解にも役立つことに注目してみましょう。

Vocabulary Quiz

次の語句の意味を a. ～ j. から選び、( ) 内に記号を記入しましょう。

1. engagement   (　　)   a. 長時間ダンス
2. volunteerism   (　　)   b. 自発的活動
3. donate   (　　)   c. 見込まれる
4. nursing home   (　　)   d. 知り合い
5. resident   (　　)   e. 寄付する
6. dance marathon (　　)   f. 誓う
7. prospective   (　　)   g. 明示された
8. acquaintance   (　　)   h. 従事
9. pledge   (　　)   i. 居住者
10. designated   (　　)   j. 介護施設

Reading

太字の語句に注意して、以下の英文を読みましょう。

1. Many Americans are future-oriented and believe in the importance of contributing to society. Consequently, many people are actively involved in social improvement through **engagement** in volunteer activities. **Volunteerism** or the practice of **donating** personal time, skills, or money to a worthwhile activity is an important American cultural value, and people's humanitarian contributions have positively impacted both the US and foreign cultures.

2. People can volunteer their time, skills, or money to a charitable organization. **Nursing homes** and hospitals are two popular volunteer venues. A nursing home volunteer could serve as a personal companion to an elderly person, share a special skill such as music or art, or read to a **resident**. Hospital volunteers visit patients and sometimes entertain them.

3. As younger people tend to enjoy activity, many volunteer through participation in a physical activity such as a charity or **dance marathon**. For example, some high schools and colleges organize an annual charity dance marathon. In order to participate in the marathon, a **prospective** dancer must raise a certain amount of money. In order to do this, the dancer solicits donations from his or her friends, **acquaintances**, and sometimes strangers. A donor agrees to **pledge** a certain amount of money for each hour the person dances. The marathoner dances for a **designated** amount of time, which is usually around twelve hours, and then collects the donation money sometime after the event. The proceeds of the marathon are then donated to a voluntary organization such as the American Cancer Society.

4. Some young people choose to volunteer at a government-sponsored organization such as the Americorps or the Peace Corps. The goal of the Americorps program is to assist with the improvement of local communities. Program participants typically volunteer for a year or more in the areas of education, public safety, health care, and environmental protection. For example, education volunteers work in underachieving schools where they tutor students and offer additional academic support. Peace Corps volunteers serve in foreign countries as teachers, health and agriculture volunteers, and so on. The goal of the program is not only to help people in developing countries but also increase their understanding of American culture. In the process of volunteering, volunteers also heighten their own intercultural awareness.

Notes

future-oriented「未来志向の」 humanitarian「人道的な」 charitable「慈善の」 solicit「懇願する」 heighten「高める」 intercultural awareness「異文化交流への自覚」

Comprehension

本文の内容に合う文になるよう、最も適切な選択肢を1つ選びましょう。

1. Americans are focused on _____ .
   a. the past
   b. the present
   c. the future
   d. none of the above

2. Many Americans want to make a _____ .
   a. social contribution
   b. political contribution
   c. high salary
   d. social involvement

3. Which of the following venues would an American most likely **not** volunteer at?
   a. A shopping mall.
   b. An orphanage.
   c. A homeless shelter.
   d. An after-school program.

4. In order to join a dance marathon, the participant must _____ .
   a. collect a certain amount of donations
   b. pay an entrance fee
   c. pass a physical examination
   d. pass a competitive selection process

5. By volunteering abroad, a person can _____ .
   a. learn how difficult it is to communicate in English
   b. experience poverty firsthand
   c. discover that Japan is one of the best places to live
   d. increase their knowledge of another culture

Dialogue

次の会話の音声を聞いて、ペアで練習をしてみましょう。

Kate: Many Americans enjoy doing volunteer work. How about Japanese people?

Yuta: Japanese people tend to volunteer at the local level, in neighborhood associations.

Kate: That's interesting. Do people volunteer in other ways?

Yuta: Table for Two was started in Japan to help address nutrition problems.

Kate: How does it work?

Yuta: School or corporate cafeterias offer diners certain nutritionally-balanced dishes. These healthy meals are identified by a TFT logo and a twenty-five yen surcharge is added to the meal cost. TFT uses the donations to provide school lunches for children in developing countries. Basically, "extra calories" from Japan are transferred to disadvantaged children.

Kate: That's great. I think young people in both countries possess a strong desire to help others and contribute to society.

Yuta: I agree.

Notes

surcharge「追加料金」

Listening Comprehension

音声を聞き、上のDialogueの内容に合う最も適切な選択肢を1つ選びましょう。

1. Japanese people prefer to help _____.
   a.
   b.
   c.

2. The goal of Table for Two is _____.
   a.
   b.
   c.

Useful Expressions

次の日本文の意味になるように、適切なものを選んで英文を完成させましょう。

1. ジョンは、勤勉であることの重要性を確信しています。
   John _____ the importance of hard work.
   a. believes in   c. thinks
   b. believes about   d. feels about

2. 彼女は、ボランティア組織に加わることを通じて障害のある子供達を助けました。
   She helped disadvantaged children through her _____ a volunteer organization.
   a. commitment around   c. participation in
   b. commitment in   d. participation about

3. その学生は、ボランティア組織に加わっています。
   The student is _____ a volunteer organization.
   a. involves   c. participates
   b. involved in   d. participated in

4. ジムは、転職することによって、真の仕事を見つけたばかりでなく、家族と余暇を過ごすために生活の優先事項を再構築しました。
   Through changing careers, Jim _____ found his true vocation but also re-ordered his life priorities to spend additional time with his family.
   a. not only   c. yet
   b. both   d. as well as

5. 若者の多くは、社会に貢献したいという強い願望を持っています。
   Many young people have a strong desire to _____ to society.
   a. make a contribution   c. do contrition
   b. find service   d. make a donation

Discussion Topics

以下のトピックについて、グループで話し合ってみましょう。

1. Discuss any volunteer activities you are involved in or would like to participate in.
2. Do you think that Japanese are more or less inclined to volunteer than Americans? Explain your opinion.
3. Why do you think that many Japanese students prefer to spend a year abroad studying English rather than doing volunteer work?

Unit 11

Context and Communication

コミュニケーションは、言語だけでなく、顔の表情や声の抑揚などの非言語的な要素によっても行われます。アメリカの文化人類学者のE・ホールは、共通の情報密度として「コンテクスト」という概念を用いて世界の文化を分析しました。コミュニケーションが、コンテクストの高低によって影響されることにも注目してみましょう。

Vocabulary Quiz

次の語句の意味を a. ～ j. から選び、( ) 内に記号を記入しましょう。

1. transmit	( )	a.	取り囲む
2. encompass	( )	b.	絶対的な
3. accomplish	( )	c.	暗黙の
4. implication	( )	d.	明白に
5. subtle	( )	e.	推測
6. explicitly	( )	f.	意思不疎通
7. implicit	( )	g.	伝える
8. inference	( )	h.	遂行する
9. absolute	( )	i.	微妙な
10. communication breakdown	( )	j.	含蓄

Reading

太字の語句に注意して、以下の英文を読みましょう。

[1]　Communication refers to how individuals **transmit** information through the use of verbal and non-verbal codes. Communication can occur face-to-face as well as through computers and writing. Language is one mode of communication that **encompasses** word choice and intonation which collectively convey meaning. For example, a speaker can communicate sarcasm through intonation. Non-verbal signals include body language, facial expression, and gesture which also transmit meaning. Individuals draw on verbal and non-verbal language in order to **accomplish** certain actions and create various social identities.

[2]　Edward Hall developed the concept of "context" in relation to culture. Hall distinguished between "high" and "low" context cultures. Speakers from high context cultures share a common cultural background, language, and communication norms. Since implicit communication (*ishin denshin*) is common in the high context Japanese culture, speakers expect that others understand the **implications** and **subtle** nuances of language. Therefore, rather than **explicitly** conveying meaning, speakers rely on vague expressions and indirectness. Since this communications style constitutes the norm, an interlocutor can interpret the message of such **implicit** communication.

[3]　In contrast, the US is considered a low context culture. Low context cultures tend to be more ethnically diverse, so speakers possess dissimilar backgrounds and assumptions about communication typically diverge. In low context cultures, communication is direct and explicit, so speakers do not need to make **inferences** or interpretations about meaning in conversation.

[4]　Context is not **absolute** but always a matter of degree, so cultures are always relatively high or low context. While the US is a predominately low context culture, New York City is lower context than California, and Alaska is higher context than California. Likewise, Germany and the US are both low context cultures, but Germany is lower context than the US.

[5]　As communication rituals vary by culture, miscommunication can occur in intercultural encounters. Cultural context impacts norms that govern communication, and consequently miscommunication can occur between speakers from high and low context cultures. Context is one of many social factors that may influence communication, so we should be careful to avoid automatically attributing **communication breakdowns** to culture. Age, ethnicity/race, gender,

and geographic background all potentially impact communication.

Notes

intonation「声の抑揚」 collectively「集合的に」 sarcasm「皮肉」 facial「顔の」 nuance「微妙な差」 diverge「異なる」 predominately「顕著に」 ritual「しきたり」

Comprehension

本文の内容に合う文になるよう、最も適切な選択肢を1つ選びましょう。

1. Communication involves the transfer of _____.
   a. verbal information
   b. non-verbal information
   c. both (a) and (b)
   d. none of the above

2. In high context cultures, communication relies heavily on _____.
   a. verbal signals
   b. interpretation
   c. conveying explicit messages
   d. alternate modes of communication

3. In low context cultures, communication is _____.
   a. indirect and implicit
   b. direct and explicit
   c. unclear
   d. none of the above

4. The high/low context distinction is _____.
   a. definite
   b. indefinite
   c. static
   d. irrelevant

5. The differences between high/low context culture is _____.
   a. the main source of miscommunication
   b. one potential cause of miscommunication
   c. unrelated to miscommunication
   d. often ignored

Dialogue

次の会話の音声を聞いて、ペアで練習をしてみましょう。

Don: A bunch of us are going out this weekend. Do you want to come?
Yuki: [Silence]. I'll think about it.
Don: Okay, let me know.

On the telephone:

Yuki: Hello?
Don: Hi Yuki. It's Don.
Yuki: Hi Don.
Don: Since I haven't heard back from you about the weekend, I decided to call you. Do you want to join us this weekend?
Yuki: [Silence] That's going to be a little bit difficult.
Don: Do you think you can come or not?
Yuki: [Silence] I already have plans.
Don: I see. I hope you can join us next time.
Yuki: I would like that very much.

Listening Comprehension

音声を聞き、上のDialogueの内容に合う最も適切な選択肢を1つ選びましょう。

1. Don _____ Yuki to go out this weekend.
   a.
   b.
   c.

2. Yuki _____ Don's invitation.
   a.
   b.
   c.

Useful Expressions

次の日本文の意味になるように、適切なものを選んで英文を完成させましょう。

1. 異文化間のコミュニケーションの不備は、文化に基づく誤解に起因しています。

    Intercultural miscommunication _____ culturally-based misunderstandings.
    - a. refers
    - b. refers to
    - c. are
    - d. have

2. コミュニケーションに関して、日本語の会話は、しばしば遠回しになります。

    In _____ communication, Japanese conversations are often indirect.
    - a. connection
    - b. connected to
    - c. relation to
    - d. relation for

3. 合衆国は、高度に個人的な文化であると見なされています。

    The United States is _____ a highly individualistic culture.
    - a. consider
    - b. considered
    - c. considerate
    - d. regarding

4. 文化は、静的なものではなく、時間を経て変化します。

    Culture is not static _____ changes over time.
    - a. but
    - b. however
    - c. never
    - d. consequently

5. アメリカ人は、直接的なコミュニケーションを好む傾向があります。

    Americans _____ prefer direct communication.
    - a. tend to
    - b. tendency
    - c. inclination
    - d. inclined to

Discussion Topics

以下のトピックについて、グループで話し合ってみましょう。

1. This unit discusses how the US is a low context culture. Do you think that you would enjoy living in this type of culture? Explain your opinion.
2. Discuss the appealing and unappealing aspects of living in a high-context culture such as present-day Japan.
3. Do you think that it is easy for miscommunication to occur between people from a low context and high context culture? Explain your opinion.

Unit 12

Non-Verbal Communication

時間の考え方も文化により異なり、時間の流れを 1 つと捉える monochronic「単時系」の文化と、複数あると捉える polychronic「複時系」の文化に大別できます。日本やアメリカの文化は前者の傾向があり、時間自体が貴重ですが、南米やアラブの文化は後者で、時間は人間関係に従属します。同じ系統の文化でも時間の扱いに違いが出ることに注目してみましょう。

Vocabulary Quiz

次の語句の意味を a. ～ j. から選び、( ) 内に記号を記入しましょう。

1. precious commodity ( ) a. 遅れた
2. agenda ( ) b. 維持する
3. metaphor ( ) c. 状況
4. alternate route ( ) d. 指定された
5. sustain ( ) e. 予定表
6. circumstance ( ) f. 比喩
7. corporate world ( ) g. 企業界
8. tardy ( ) h. 怒らせる
9. offend ( ) i. 代わりの道
10. specified ( ) j. 貴重品

Reading

太字の語句に注意して、以下の英文を読みましょう。

1 The perception and use of time varies by culture. Compared to other cultures, punctuality is vital in the US and Japan. Time is regarded as a **precious commodity** that should not be wasted. On the other hand, there are cultures where punctuality is less important, so lateness is the norm. As people are often unconscious about how they perceive and use time, such differences can result in intercultural miscommunication.

2 The US and Japan follow a monochronic time system. Monochronic societies regard time as a tangible and extremely valuable resource. Punctuality is venerated and schedules or **agendas** are strictly followed. American English has several **metaphors** that demonstrate the high value placed on time. Time is saved, spent, wasted, lost, killed, or running out. For example, "we wasted an hour looking for the restaurant" or "we saved an hour by taking this **alternate route**." Likewise, the expression "show up on time" reflects the importance of punctuality in Japan.

3 A polychronic time system is another way to conceptualize time. Polychronic societies view time abstractly and their lives are not driven by the clock. Building and **sustaining** interpersonal relationships is extremely important to polychronic people, so they place a higher value on spending time with family and friends than arriving for an appointment on time. Latin American and Arabic cultures are examples of polychronic societies.

4 Cultures are not always easily classifiable as "monochronic" or "polychronic." In reality, a culture can follow both time systems in different **circumstances**. For instance, North American Indians follow a polychronic time system, and time is more polychronic in the Southeast part of the US than in the Northeast. Likewise, Japan is overwhelmingly more monochronically-oriented than the US. While public transportation is frequently late in the US, it runs precisely on time in Japan. In many circumstances, the tolerance for lateness is much higher in the US than in Japan. In the US **corporate world**, however, the metaphor "time is money" is the modus operandi, so punctuality is the norm. In sum, monochronic and polychronic represent the opposite ends of a continuum and cultures exist as points on the continuum.

5 Clearly, the way a culture frames time could contribute to intercultural communication breakdowns. For instance, an American exchange student who

is frequently **tardy** to meetings and appointments could unknowingly **offend** Japanese people. On the other hand, a Japanese exchange student who arrives to a party at the **specified** start time may find that he/she is the first guest to arrive and feel foolish.

Notes

punctuality「時間厳守」 monochronic「単時系の（時間の流れは一つの）」（Edward Hallの造語） tangible「触れることの出来る、現実の」 venerate「大切にする」 polychronic「複時系の（時間の流れは複数の）」（Edward Hallの造語） overwhelmingly「圧倒的に」 modus operandi「仕事の流儀」 continuum「連続」

Comprehension

本文の内容に合う文になるよう、最も適切な選択肢を1つ選びましょう。

1. In both Japan and the US, punctuality is _____.
   a. valued
   b. overvalued
   c. undervalued
   d. unimportant

2. In polychronically-oriented cultures, building human relationships is _____.
   a. important
   b. unimportant
   c. unusual
   d. inappropriate

3. In monochronically-oriented cultures, time is regarded as _____.
   a. transparent
   b. ambiguous
   c. tangible
   d. an abstract concept

4. The monochronic/polychronic time distinction is _____.
   a. absolute
   b. not absolute
   c. static
   d. irrelevant

5. A culture's time system is _____.
   a. the main source of miscommunication
   b. one potential cause of miscommunication
   c. unrelated to miscommunication
   d. unimportant

Dialogue

次の会話の音声を聞いて、ペアで練習をしてみましょう。

Becky: I bet living in the US is a big adjustment. How are you holding up?

Ryo: Pretty good, but I want to ask you about something.

Becky: Sure.

Ryo: I was invited to a party last week. I arrived right on time, but people started rolling in late.

Becky: Regarding parties, American college students are fairly easy going. Most people don't want to be the first guest to arrive at a party, so they come a bit late. We call people who are noticeably late "fashionably late" because they give the impression that they are very busy and popular people and unable to arrive on time.

Ryo: I see. We often say "arrive five minutes early" in Japanese, but I guess punctuality is less important in the US

Becky: College students are quite laid back and unpunctual, but you should be on time for formal appointments, meetings, and job interviews. The world outside of college is more unforgiving.

Ryo: Thanks for the tip!

Becky: Don't mention it.

Listening Comprehension

音声を聞き、上のDialogueの内容に合う最も適切な選択肢を1つ選びましょう。

1. Ryo asks Becky about _____.
   a.
   b.
   c.

2. In the business world, punctuality is _____.
   a.
   b.
   c.

Useful Expressions

次の日本文の意味になるように、適切なものを選んで英文を完成させましょう。

1. ユキは、コンピュータで2時間無駄にしてしまいました。

    Yuki _____ two hours on the computer.
    - a. run out
    - b. contributed
    - c. were
    - d. wasted

2. 日本は、単時系志向の文化で、時計に追われています。

    Japan is a monochronic time-oriented culture and thus is _____ by the clock.
    - a. made
    - b. possessed
    - c. driven
    - d. spent

3. アメリカの文化は、自信を非常に重要なものと見なします。

    American culture _____ self-confidence as extremely important.
    - a. motto
    - b. regards
    - c. view
    - d. cares

4. その学生は、6ヶ月アメリカに住んで、うまく持ちこたえています。

    The student has lived in the US for six months and is _____ quite well.
    - a. interrupted
    - b. preparing
    - c. holding out
    - d. holding up

5. パーティーは1時間前に始まりましたが、ジャックは今ようやく辿り着くところです。

    The party started an hour ago, but Jack is just _____ now.
    - a. rolling over
    - b. rolling in
    - c. arrived
    - d. holding out

Discussion Topics

以下のトピックについて、グループで話し合ってみましょう。

1. Do you think that you would enjoy living in a polychronic time-oriented culture? Explain your opinion.
2. Japan is a very monochronic time-oriented culture. Discuss the positive and negative effects of this time system.
3. Do you think that it is easy for miscommunication to occur between people from a monochronic time-oriented and polychronic time-oriented culture? Explain your opinion.

Unit 13

Debate

　アメリカ文化の中では相手を論破することが重視され、社会問題についての激論を取り上げるテレビ番組があったり、中等教育でも明確な自己主張が求められています。自己弁護が強まると問題の精査や他人の意見の理解がないがしろにされます。調和を求め、意見対立を回避しようとする日本文化との違いに注目してみましょう。

Vocabulary Quiz

次の語句の意味を a. ～ j. から選び、( ) 内に記号を記入しましょう。

1. controversial　　　　(　)　　a. 交際する
2. social issues　　　　(　)　　b. 激しく
3. spark　　　　　　　(　)　　c. 論争の的となる
4. plagued　　　　　　(　)　　d. 妨げられた
5. fiercely　　　　　　(　)　　e. 無価値にする
6. underresearched　　　(　)　　f. ～の引き金となる
7. invalidated　　　　　(　)　　g. 十分に調査されていない
8. disagreement　　　　(　)　　h. 浸食された
9. hedged　　　　　　　(　)　　i. 社会問題
10. socialize　　　　　　(　)　　j. 意見対立

Reading

太字の語句に注意して、以下の英文を読みましょう。

[1]　From an early age, American children learn the importance of formulating and supporting an opinion. The media disseminates images of people debating various **controversial social issues** such as abortion, capital punishment, and gun control. These issues are controversial because they **spark** heated public discussions and debates. The topics are frequently the subject of debate in many secondary school classrooms. In US culture, having and defending an opinion is more important than the accuracy of the opinion, and those who cannot express an opinion are regarded as incompetent. Consequently, many Americans are eager to share and even debate their opinions with others.

[2]　Sociolinguist Deborah Tannen maintains that American culture is **plagued** by the tendency to frame most issues in the form of a debate rather than a dialogue. Tannen's term for this phenomenon is an "argument" culture. Accordingly, individuals assume either an affirmative "pro" stance or negative "anti" stance in relation to many controversial social issues. The argument culture does not reward the ability to recognize the opposite position or even modify one's own position. Rather, the society validates the ability to **fiercely** defend one's own position at all costs.

[3]　The argumentative environment that Tannen describes extends to the classroom. In many classrooms, students engage in heated debates about issues. Since winning is the main objective of these debates, students' arguments are often **underresearched** and weak rather than well-researched and solid. Another unfortunate consequence of the argument culture is that the adversarial communication style dominates the classroom and diverse communication styles are **invalidated**.

[4]　As Japanese culture values the maintenance of harmony, direct **disagreement** would have a detrimental effect on interpersonal relationships. Therefore, disagreement tends to be mitigated, **hedged**, and even avoided rather than explicit and direct. Although students passionately debate issues in the classroom in the US, disagreement on these issues does not damage their relationships. In fact, students commonly **socialize** and form friendships with others who disagree on many topics.

Notes

disseminate「広める」 incompetent「能力のない」 sociolinguist「社会言語学者」 affirmative「肯定的な」 validate「有効にする」 argumentative「議論好きの」 adversarial「敵対的な」 detrimental「損害となる」 mitigated「緩和された」 passionately「激しく」

Comprehension

本文の内容に合う文になるよう、最も適切な選択肢を1つ選びましょう。

1. American culture prizes the ability to _____.
   a. have an opinion
   b. defend an opinion
   c. both a. and b.
   d. formulate a well-researched opinion

2. In an argument culture, _____.
   a. debate is more important than dialogue
   b. dialogue is more important than debate
   c. debate and dialogue are equally valued
   d. debate and dialogue are undervalued

3. Many secondary school classrooms reward the ability to _____.
   a. present a well-researched argument
   b. cooperate with others
   c. acknowledge the opposing position
   d. defend an argument at all costs

4. In classrooms that reward an adversarial communication style, _____.
   a. alternative communication styles are equally valued
   b. this style is not dominate
   c. students learn to respect other communication styles
   d. other communication styles are viewed as invalid

5. In Japan, direct disagreement can _____.
   a. build solidarity between people
   b. create rapport between people
   c. repair interpersonal relationships
   d. damage interpersonal relationships

Unit 13 Debate

Dialogue

次の会話の音声を聞いて、ペアで練習をしてみましょう。

David: I oppose capital punishment because the murder of all human beings is morally wrong.

Chihiro: We can both agree that murder is wrong; however, I think that criminals who commit murder deserve to die.

David: The government sometimes wrongfully executes innocent individuals. For this reason alone, capital punishment should be abolished.

Chihiro: You are referring to an extremely small number of people. By executing the murderer, the victims' families can feel at ease. They no longer have to worry that the criminal will be released from prison or not receive punishment.

David: The family can also feel at ease when a criminal receives the sentence of life imprisonment without parole.

Chihiro: I know that we'll never see eye to eye on this issue, but I enjoyed the debate.

David: I did too. I'm starving. Let's grab a bite to eat.

Chihiro: Sounds great.

Listening Comprehension

音声を聞き、上のDialogueの内容に合う最も適切な選択肢を1つ選びましょう。

1. Chihiro and David discuss _____.
    a.
    b.
    c.

2. After the debate, Chihiro and David's relationship is _____.
    a.
    b.
    c.

Useful Expressions

次の日本文の意味になるように、適切なものを選んで英文を完成させましょう。

1. 最近の学校での銃撃は、銃規制の法律に関する大衆の激しい議論を引き起こしました。

    The recent school shooting _____ a heated public debate about gun control laws.

    a. fired
    b. suppressed
    c. sparked
    d. developed

2. その政治家は、どんなことをしても間近になっている選挙に勝利する決意をしています。

    The politician is determined to win the upcoming election _____ costs.

    a. at every
    b. at all
    c. with
    d. for

3. その学生は、カナダかアメリカのどちらかに留学することを決めるでしょう。

    The student will decide to study abroad in _____ Canada _____ the United States.

    a. either; or
    b. but; also
    c. neither; nor
    d. only; but

4. 彼らは、その問題について意見が一致しませんでしたが、友達のままでいました。

    Even though they could not see _____ on the issue, they remained friends.

    a. eye to eye
    b. the same
    c. the view
    d. for

5. 授業の後、学生達は軽食を取りました。

    After class, the students _____ a bite to eat.

    a. grabbed
    b. gained
    c. have
    d. picked up

Discussion Topics

以下のトピックについて、グループで話し合ってみましょう。

1. Discuss the positive and negative aspects of an "argument" culture.
2. Do you think that you would enjoy living in an "argument" culture such as the United States? Explain your opinion.
3. Do you think that Japanese should learn how to debate?

Unit 14

Religion

　宗教は生死についての信念を表したものですが、アメリカの人口の約8割の人がキリスト教に何らかの信仰心を抱いています。合衆国憲法では信仰の自由が保障されていて、様々な宗教が影響力を発揮しています。アメリカは、世俗的な国になっていると言われますが、先進工業国の中で最も宗教的な国であることに注目してみましょう。

Vocabulary Quiz

次の語句の意味を a. ～ j. から選び、( ) 内に記号を記入しましょう。

1. eternal salvation	( )	a.	移住する
2. migrate	( )	b.	おおよそ
3. roughly	( )	c.	発揮する
4. fundamental	( )	d.	重要ではない
5. enduring	( )	e.	世俗的な
6. prohibit	( )	f.	永遠の救済
7. discriminate	( )	g.	根本的な
8. exert	( )	h.	禁止する
9. secular	( )	i.	差別する
10. unimportant	( )	j.	恒久的な

Reading

太字の語句に注意して、以下の英文を読みましょう。

1   A religion is a belief system about the origins and purpose of life which is typically underpinned by a belief in the existence of a supernatural being such as God. The purpose of religion is to provide individuals with a moral code that guides their lives as well as offer hope for **eternal salvation**. Religion has a long history in American culture and continues to play a critical role there.

2   Many early settlers **migrated** to North America because they experienced religious persecution in England. Although the United States is a diverse nation, Christianity remains the dominant religion. **Roughly** 80 percent of the population affiliates with the Christian faith. As nearly 25 percent of the US population identifies with the Roman Catholic Christian faith, this is the single largest denomination. Christians believe that Jesus Christ is God's son and that following his teachings will lead to eternal salvation. Other religions are practiced in the US such as Judaism, Buddhism, Islam, and Hinduism, but their influence is significantly less than Christianity's influence.

3   Religious freedom is a **fundamental** and **enduring** value in American culture. The First Amendment to the US Constitution provides citizens with the right to freely practice or not practice religion. For instance, school absences due to religious observations are permissible. Similarly, federal law **prohibits** religious discrimination regarding any aspect of employment. As religious freedom is a founding principle of the US, Americans can freely practice or reject religion and people cannot be **discriminated** against due to their religious or nonreligious beliefs and practices.

4   Some may argue that the significance of religion is declining in the US, but Christianity has **exerted** a long-lasting impact on American and European cultures, and its influence is still evident today. A **secular** society is one where religion is absent from many aspects of daily life and thus regarded as **unimportant**. Among industrialized nations, the US is one of the most churchgoing societies, so a claim that the US is a secular society is inaccurate. Christianity has influenced art, education, science, and medicine, and references to Christianity can be found in popular films and music. In addition to Christianity's cultural influence, practicing Christians' charitable work contributes to the improvement of societies worldwide. For instance, the Catholic Church is the most charitable organization worldwide and provides food, shelter, and education to the

underprivileged and impoverished regardless of their religious affiliation.

Notes

underpinned「下から支えられた (underpinの過去分詞形)」 supernatural「超自然的な」 persecution「迫害」 affiliate「所属する」 denomination「教派、教団」 First Amendment「憲法修正第1条」 churchgoing「定期的に教会へ行く」 inaccurate「不正確な」 charitable「慈善を行う」 underprivileged「恵まれない」 impoverished「貧困の」 affiliation「所属」

Comprehension

本文の内容に合う文になるよう、最も適切な選択肢を1つ選びましょう。

1. The purpose of religion is _____.
   a. to teach morals
   b. to provide hope of an afterlife
   c. both a. and b.
   d. none of the above

2. Europeans immigrated to North America to escape from _____.
   a. diseases
   b. high taxes
   c. the monarchy
   d. religious oppression

3. Which of the following is the dominant religion in the US?
   a. Christianity.
   b. Judaism.
   c. Islam.
   d. None of the above.

4. According to the passage, the US Constitution guarantees _____.
   a. voting rights
   b. religious persecution
   c. religious freedom
   d. none of the above

5. Secularism is _____.
   a. exerting a strong influence on US society
   b. present but not exerting a strong influence on US society
   c. dominant in US society
   d. important in American culture

Dialogue

次の会話の音声を聞いて、ペアで練習をしてみましょう。

John: Our family attends a church service every Sunday. Would you like to join us this weekend?

Emi: What do you do at church?

John: We sing, pray, and listen to readings from the Bible.

Emi: I see. That sounds interesting.

John: People go to church and practice a religion for different reasons. For me, religion offers a moral code to live my life and gives me hope of an afterlife.

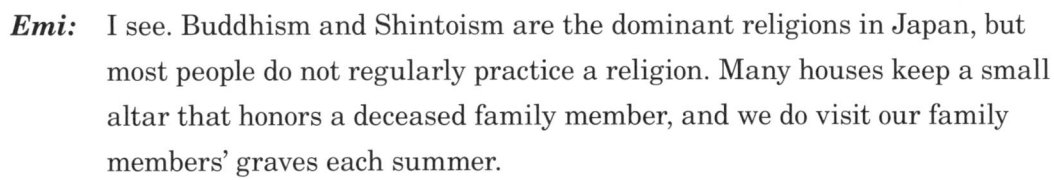

Emi: I see. Buddhism and Shintoism are the dominant religions in Japan, but most people do not regularly practice a religion. Many houses keep a small altar that honors a deceased family member, and we do visit our family members' graves each summer.

John: It sounds like Japanese people have a belief in an afterlife, so they are not atheist. How do you feel about Sunday?

Emi: I really appreciate the invitation, but my preference is not to attend.

John: That's fine. Let me know if you change your mind.

Emi: I will. Thanks for understanding.

Notes

altar「祭壇」 atheist「無神論者」

Listening Comprehension

音声を聞き、上のDialogueの内容に合う最も適切な選択肢を1つ選びましょう。

1. John practices a religion because _____.
    a.
    b.
    c.

2. According to Emi, Japanese people are _____.
    a.
    b.
    c.

Useful Expressions

次の日本文の意味になるように、適切なものを選んで英文を完成させましょう。

1. サラは新しい仕事に就いたので、もう以前の会社には所属していません。
    Since Sarah got a new job, she is no longer _____ her former company
    a. connected
    b. affiliated
    c. affiliated with
    d. linked

2. 仏教と神道は日本文化の中で重要な役割を果たしていますが、多くの人は特定の宗教との結び付きを明らかにしたりしません。
    While Shintoism and Buddhism play an important role in Japanese culture, many people do not _____ a particular religion.
    a. connect to
    b. identify for
    c. identify
    d. identify with

3. 学生食堂は、学生達に食事の多くの選択肢を提供します。
    The school cafeteria _____ students _____ many meal choices.
    a. provides; with
    b. provides; for
    c. encourages; to
    d. discourages; from

4. アメリカ人は外国語の学習に興味を持っていないと論じる人もいます。
    One may _____ Americans are uninterested in learning foreign languages.
    a. argue with
    b. argue that
    c. promote that
    d. agree for

5. 世界の国々の中で、日本はとても豊かな国の1つです。
    _____ world nations, Japan is a very wealthy nation.
    a. Over
    b. In the midst
    c. However
    d. Among

Discussion Topics

以下のトピックについて、グループで話し合ってみましょう。

1. What events or daily practices show Christianity's influence?
2. Who do Japanese people consider as the final judge of moral and immoral behavior?
3. One could argue that the fear of God or hell is the reason why many people act morally. Do you think that the fear of shame or embarrassment guides Japanese people's behavior? Explain your opinion.

Unit 15

Computers and Communication

情報機器の発展に伴い、今日ではコンピュータ媒介伝達（CMC）が増えています。顔を合わせて会話する時には話者の表情や動作などが意味を補ったりしますが、CMC では表現された言葉が全てで、誤解の度合いが大きくなります。CMC が抱える問題点、特に英語学習者が CMC を行う時の課題に注目してみましょう。

Vocabulary Quiz

次の語句の意味を a.～j. から選び、（ ）内に記号を記入しましょう。

1. computer-mediated communication （　　）　　a. 未知の
2. onset （　　）　　b. 誤伝達
3. addiction （　　）　　c. コンピュータ媒介伝達
4. overreliance （　　）　　d. 受け手
5. irrelevant （　　）　　e. 誤って解釈する
6. cyberspace （　　）　　f. 開始
7. miscommunication （　　）　　g. 不適切な
8. recipient （　　）　　h. 電脳空間
9. misinterpret （　　）　　i. 過剰依存
10. unfamiliar （　　）　　j. 熱中

Reading

太字の語句に注意して、以下の英文を読みましょう。

1　In the current digital age, communication occurs through not only the traditional channels of speech and writing but also via computers. **Computer-mediated communication (CMC)** enables people to instantaneously communicate with others from around the globe. Computers give users access to a wealth of information and are invaluable language-learning tools. However, there are also a number of disadvantages associated with CMC.

2　The **onset** of the digital age has drastically transformed communication. Communication no longer occurs exclusively face-to-face or over the phone but through text messages, e-mail, and social media. People also have access to a variety of devices such as laptop computers, smart phones, personal gaming devices, and tablets. **Addiction** can result from the **overreliance** on these devices.

3　There are some significant differences between face-to-face communication and CMC. Face-to-face communication enables speakers to observe verbal and non-verbal cues and respond immediately. Speakers are also expected to observe social norms and appropriate ways of social interaction. In some forms of computer-mediated communication, observing the appropriate ways of social interaction is largely **irrelevant**. As interlocutors exist in **cyberspace**, individuals can send inappropriate or impolite messages to others through social media. Without face-to-face interaction, people do not acquire crucial social skills and could become antisocial.

4　The potential for **miscommunication** is higher in CMC than face-to-face communication. Individuals can experience difficulty deciphering their interlocutor's intended meaning through CMC. In text-messaging or online chatting, the **recipient** can easily **misinterpret** a message's meaning because the person interprets the message without access to the sender's intended tone, body language, and facial expression. Likewise, one can misunderstand the meaning of a Twitter tweet. The abbreviated format of messages also increases the likelihood of miscommunication.

5　The probability of miscommunication is substantially higher between a native English and native Japanese speaker. For example, if they are communicating in English, the Japanese speaker is expected to not only decipher the computer mediated message's meaning but also attempt to decode the nuances of a message

in their second language. A Japanese speaker may be **unfamiliar** with a certain
35 expression or slang term that is unique to American English. The Japanese speaker also has to interpret this unfamiliar term without the assistance of tone, body language, and facial expression.

Notes
instantaneously「瞬時に」 drastically「劇的に」 antisocial「反社会的な」 decipher「解読する」
facial「顔の」 abbreviated「短縮された」 decode「(信号を元に戻して) 読み取る」

Comprehension

本文の内容に合う文になるよう、最も適切な選択肢を1つ選びましょう。

1. The current digital age has _____.
   a. altered communication
   b. shared communication
   c. left communication unaffected
   d. made communication more inconvenient

2. Face-to-face communication is _____.
   a. mostly verbal
   b. largely non-verbal
   c. both verbal and non-verbal
   d. extinct

3. The spread of CMC _____.
   a. enhances the development of social skills
   b. decreases the development of social skills
   c. is slowing
   d. has no impact on the development of social skills

4. Miscommunication can result from a CMC encounter because individuals _____.
   a. correctly interpret the meaning of a message
   b. ignore the meaning of a message
   c. may misinterpret the meaning of a message
   d. are unfamiliar with this mode of communication

5. The probability of miscommunication between speakers with different native languages is higher because speakers may _____.
   a. decode the implications of a message
   b. avoid face-to-face communication
   c. misinterpret the implications of a message
   d. depend on CMC

Dialogue

次の会話の音声を聞いて、ペアで練習をしてみましょう。

Derek: We had an interesting discussion about cell phones and social media in class.

Nozomi: What did you discuss?

Derek: We talked about how people are engrossed in their mobile devices.

Nozomi: The situation is similar in Japan. People are always texting or using social media while on the train or even in class.

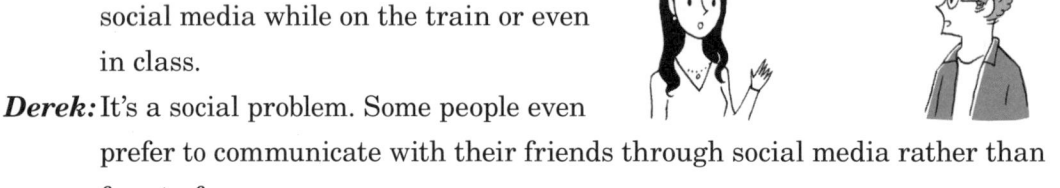

Derek: It's a social problem. Some people even prefer to communicate with their friends through social media rather than face-to-face.

Nozomi: That's crazy, but I can believe it. I regularly use mobile devices, but I think we need to be careful not to overuse these devices and become dependent on them.

Derek: I agree. People need to be careful that they do not become addicted to this technology.

Listening Comprehension

音声を聞き、上のDialogueの内容に合う最も適切な選択肢を1つ選びましょう。

1. Mobile device usage _____ .

    a.
    b.
    c.

2. Which detrimental health effect does the dialogue discuss?

    a.
    b.
    c.

Useful Expressions

次の日本文の意味になるように、適切なものを選んで英文を完成させましょう。

1. インターネットは、膨大な情報を提供します。

   The internet provides a _____ of information.
   - a. generous
   - b. lack
   - c. wealth
   - d. scarcity

2. この薬の服用に結びついた副作用があります。

   There are side effects _____ this medication.
   - a. associated with
   - b. linked through
   - c. related with
   - d. connection with

3. 発熱は、しばしば風邪の始まりに先立って出ます。

   A fever often precedes the _____ of a cold.
   - a. end
   - b. introduction
   - c. begin
   - d. onset

4. 電子辞書は、言語学習には計り知れないほど貴重な道具です。

   Electronic dictionaries are _____ tool for language learning.
   - a. an unclear
   - b. a useless
   - c. a wasteful
   - d. an invaluable

5. ビデオ会議は、人々が世界の異なった地域からコミュニケーションをとれるようにします。

   Videoconferencing _____ people to communicate from different parts of the world.
   - a. for
   - b. able
   - c. disables
   - d. enables

Discussion Topics

以下のトピックについて、グループで話し合ってみましょう。

1. People have access to a variety of digital devices today. Which devices do you use? When do you feel they are useful?
2. Digital devices provide access to a number of social networking services (SNS). Which SNS do you use? Discuss the positive and negative aspects of SNS.
3. Discuss aspects of CMC that could lead to intercultural miscommunication.

本書にはCD（別売）があります

Cultural Portraits: Japan and the US
日米文化比較で学ぶ総合英語

2015年1月20日　初版第1刷発行
2025年2月20日　初版第9刷発行

著　者　　Justin Charlebois
　　　　　佐久間　重

発行者　　福　岡　正　人
発行所　　株式会社　金　星　堂
（〒101-0051）東京都千代田区神田神保町3-21
Tel. (03) 3263-3828（営業部）
　　 (03) 3263-3997（編集部）
Fax (03) 3263-0716
https://www.kinsei-do.co.jp

編集担当　芦川正宏　　　　　　　　　Printed in Japan
印刷所・製本所／倉敷印刷株式会社
本書の無断複製・複写は著作権法上での例外を除き禁じられています。
本書を代行業者等の第三者に依頼してスキャンやデジタル化すること
は、たとえ個人や家庭内での利用であっても認められておりません。
落丁・乱丁本はお取り替えいたします。

ISBN978-4-7647-3998-7　C1082